"Plant-based cuisine that is inventive, flavorful, fun and above all else, accessible to the masses. You will fall in love with Dustin's approachable recipes that flourish with familiar ingredients we all know and love. Not just for vegans, everyone will enjoy this over-the-top spin on comfort classics paired with beautiful images, personal anecdotes, and an entertaining, can-do approach!"

—Miyoko Schinner, author, television host, founder and CEO of Miyoko's Kitchen

---

"Dustin has taken his vegan creations to a whole other level! Every recipe in *Epic Vegan* starts off as a true classic, but then he puts his magical twist on it to make it unique, scrumptious, and, most importantly, very easy to make. I've been lucky enough to taste-test all of these recipes and, let me tell you, they are amazing! What's not to drool over in his Almost Famous Buffalo Chicken Lasagna and Pumpkin Cream Cheese Latte Shake? His Double-Stacked Cookie Dough Cake had me begging for more!"

—Chloe Coscarelli, vegan chef and author of *Chloe Flavor*

"Every*one* is going to be able to cook, create, and bake every*thing* they have been craving, *sans* animal products. And, they'll be healthier, happier, full, and satisfied without any excuses."

—Doron Petersan, Food Network *Cupcake Wars* champion, author of *Sticky Fingers' Vegan Sweets*, and owner of Sticky Fingers and Fare Well D.C.

"Pure vegan joy! From succulent seitan to lobster rolls in a biscuit, this treasure trove of recipes shall turn your normal dinner rotation into a vegan road trip for the ages."

—Kale Walch, The Herbivorous Butcher

"Dustin Harder throws the plant-based party of the year with *Epic Vegan*. With genius recipes (hello, Franks 'n Mac Pizza, Breakfast Nachos, and Birthday Cake Shakes) and Harder's signature humor, this cookbook is an absolute blast."

—Colleen Holland, publisher and co-founder *VegNews Magazine*

"If you have ever had an inkling or craving for some serious stunt food as a vegan, Dustin has you more than covered with *Epic Vegan*. Combinations that only a mad food scientist could come up with are executed beautifully for dishes that are guaranteed to make you salivate."

—Jackie Sobon, author of *Vegan Yack Attack On the Go!* and *Vegan Bowl Attack!*

"*Epic Vegan* is a kick-ass cookbook, breaking the stereotype that vegan food is bland, limited, and boring. A great addition to that must-have cookbook list!"

—Chad Sarno, chef, author, and co-founder of Wicked Healthy and VP Culinary Good Catch Foods

---

EPIC VEGAN

WILD AND OVER-THE-TOP PLANT-BASED RECIPES

DUSTIN HARDER

FAIR WINDS

Inspiring | Educating | Creating | Entertaining

Brimming with creative inspiration, how-to projects, and useful information to enrich your everyday life, Quarto Knows is a favorite destination for those pursuing their interests and passions. Visit our site and dig deeper with our books into your area of interest: Quarto Creates, Quarto Cooks, Quarto Homes, Quarto Lives, Quarto Drives, Quarto Explores, Quarto Gifts, or Quarto Kids.

23 22 21 20 19 3 4 5

ISBN: 978-1-59233-876-4

Digital edition published in 2019

eISBN: 978-1-63159-696-4

Library of Congress Cataloging-in-Publication Data available.

Design: www.traffic-design.co.uk
Cover Image: Luciana Pampalone
Page Layout: www.traffic-design.co.uk
Food Photography: Ashley Madden from riseshinecook.ca, @riseshinecook (except page 163 Amber Orlino)
Lifestyle Photography: Luciana Pampalone

Printed in China

The information in this book is for educational purposes only. It is not intended to replace the advice of a physician or medical practitioner. Please see your health-care provider before beginning any new health program.

This book is dedicated to all of the adults who still like to play with their food.

CONTENTS

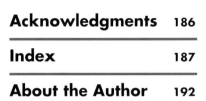

INTRODUCTION

Why This Book?

Let's get *epic*! It's time to stop taking food so seriously and letting pretentious chefs scare you out of the kitchen. It's time to play with your food. Who's with me?!

This book was heavily inspired by my travels while filming my video series *The Vegan Roadie*. During these travels, I learned many things, primarily that people are hesitant about plant-based eating because they feel it's unfamiliar, boring, or bland. Consumers have been heavily influenced by a fast-food nation with snappy ad campaigns boasting over-the-top creations. But vegans can create fun, irreverent, and exciting food too! This book is an invitation for vegans (and their nonvegan friends) to come together in the kitchen, communicate, and create.

I started *The Vegan Roadie* in 2014 after I graduated from the Natural Gourmet Institute in New York City. I had a committed mission to bridge the gap between vegans and nonvegans, to make plant-based eating accessible and welcoming, and, above all else, to entertain and make cooking or dining out a FUN experience. I have always said, "I can't get someone to go from eating double cheeseburgers to drinking green smoothies in one day. But I *can* replace that double cheeseburger with an exact replica in taste, texture, and sight." Maybe

it will ignite a spark, relieve some intimidation, and help guide that person toward a happier, healthier, and more compassionate lifestyle.

In 2007, when I was transitioning into a plant-based lifestyle, I found myself turned off from it because I felt judged within the vegan community for my past meat-and-potatoes lifestyle, and because I was eating processed animal-free foods. After muddling my way through the judgment of others, I have this advice to offer: It's about YOU. I want you to honor your journey, and for goodness sake, have some *epic fun* along the way! I applaud you for taking *any* steps, big or small, toward eliminating animal products of any kind from your diet and lifestyle. My only hope is that this book gets you excited about the possibilities that lie ahead for you.

The Epic Food

This book is greatly influenced by what is known as "stunt foods." What is a stunt food, you ask? You know when a Broadway show brings in a really big television or movie star to play a lead role in order to sell tickets? That's called "stunt casting," and "stunt food" is sort of the same thing. Crazy creations like the Dorito-shell taco at Taco Bell or the fried chicken bun at KFC serve the same purpose: to lure customers.

While plant-based restaurants are offering more stunt food or over-the-top creations to excite the masses these days, I thought it would be *epic* if you could create some stunt food of your own at home. You know—foods to wow guests at parties, put together with friends and family, and take pictures of for Instagram.

Some of these recipes truly are a marriage of wacky ideas, while others are replicas and combinations of foods that will be familiar to you from our fast-food nation.

I know the idea of building recipes on top of each other might sound intimidating, but fear not! This book starts you out with some very simple variations of classic comfort foods like macaroni and cheese, fried chicken, pizza, burgers, and donuts. Each chapter incorporates these basics, combining them to make epic stunt-food creations. So here's your chance, beginners and experts alike: Grab your apron (or your wig and high heels to turn on your inner Julia Child—whatever gets you excited in the kitchen), and get ready to create some magic. Get ready… to be EPIC.

Tools

I try to keep the kitchen tools needed in this book to a minimum—hopefully stuff you already have like basic pots, pans, cookie sheets, and so on. I'm sure it goes without saying, however, that to create truly epic vegan masterpieces, you will need more than a standard skillet at times. I encourage you to get friendly with your fellow cooks, neighbors, etc., and borrow any tools you don't have that might pop up; you might even consider starting a cooking club. I was fortunate to be part of one (shout out to my NYC plant-based buddies of 2013!), and it's what ignited my spark to create the change in the world that I wanted to see.

I do call for a high-speed blender and food processor in some recipes. If you don't already have a high-speed blender, there have been some incredible, less expensive ones to hit the market in the last few years. If you want to keep the old blender you have, that's fine too—you might just need to add a little extra liquid to get where you're going in some recipes. I use a food processor sparingly, but pulsing in a blender is a sufficient backup plan if need be.

If there is a specialty item, like a donut cutter, I do my best to offer a DIY alternative. There is always room for creativity in the kitchen!

> **After muddling my way through the judgment of others, I have this advice to offer: It's about YOU. I want you to honor your journey, and for goodness sake, have some epic fun along the way!"**

Ingredients

I get really excited about not relying on hard-to-find specialty ingredients when I create recipes. Sometimes, however, those specialty ingredients are exactly what you need to take a recipe to the next level—to be epic. I encourage you to explore any ingredients that are new to you with enthusiasm. Discovering something new I can do with plants is one of the most inspiring things I love about what I do—and I know you will love the discovery too!

In terms of sourcing, the Internet has become my best friend when I'm on the search for something and I hit a dead end at my local grocer. I also want to mention Bob's Red Mill here. You know, the jolly-looking man in a light blue cap? Many grocery stores have their own Bob's Red Mill sections, often in the baking aisle, and in natural foods sections where you can find vegan products like nutritional yeast and vital wheat gluten. And if you can't find them, kindly ask the store manager to order the items you need. You're helping yourself and the next customer who comes in looking for those items, so it's win-win. Look at the good you do!

Not Your Grandmother's Pantry

Here's a short list of some of the ingredients in this book that might be new to some of you. Most of them can be found in the natural foods or ethnic sections of well-stocked supermarkets. Don't be afraid to ask!

- Nutritional yeast
- Vital wheat gluten
- Dulse (dried red seaweed)
- Nori (dried green or black seaweed)
- Hemp seeds
- Flax meal
- Hearts of palm
- Jackfruit
- Matcha

A little note on Seitan (pronounced *say-tan*): This high protein, soy-free meat alternative made from cooking vital wheat gluten is a great substitute for products such as tofu or tempeh that contain soy, if going soy-free is your thing. Personally, I enjoy the texture of seitan a little more than tofu or tempeh when needing something of a heartier texture in a recipe. I love to use seitan in place of cauliflower in the Everything Buffalo Cauliflower Bites (page 84) when I'm feeding a room of carnivores!

Store-Bought Staples

Want to make seitan from scratch? Great—head to the Simply Seitan recipe on page 22 and be fierce! I promise you it is simple as well as functional in many of the recipes in this book. But find yourself short on time and just want to make something awesome without waiting for that seitan to cook? Good news: You can still be fierce! I support you with a tip of my hat and a round of applause. Many health food stores and even mainstream grocery stores carry packaged seitan—along with a wide variety of other vegan products—on the regular; it's just a matter of finding it! I want to take this moment to wrap my strong vegan arms gently around you for a hug and whisper this sweet nothing of a reminder in your ear: It's YOUR journey; honor it. If using these products makes life easier for you, don't feel bad; go forth and enjoy them freely! It doesn't have to be an epic day, everyday.

Here are just a few widely available vegan brands, in no particular order. Bear in mind this is not a comprehensive list. It's simply one to get you started and covers the brands I used most frequently when I tested the recipes for this book. Many are available internationally, but that changes depending on where you live and shop.

Cheese

- Chao
- Daiya
- Follow Your Heart
- Heidi Ho
- Kite Hill
- Miyoko's Creamery
- Violife

Yogurt

- Daiya
- Forager Project
- Kite Hill
- So Delicious

Cream Cheese

- Follow Your Heart
- Kite Hill
- Toffuti

Sour Cream

- Follow Your Heart
- Toffuti

Butter

- Earth Balance
- Miyoko's Creamery

Mayonnaise

- Follow Your Heart Vegenaise
- Just Mayo

Meats

▼ Beyond Meat
▼ Field Roast Grain Meat Co.
▼ Gardein
▼ Sweet Earth
▼ Tofurky
▼ Upton's Naturals

Seitan

▼ Blackbird Foods
▼ Upton's Naturals
▼ WestSoy

Ice Cream

▼ Ben & Jerry's Non-Dairy
▼ DF Mavens
▼ Luna and Larry's Coconut Bliss
▼ NadaMoo
▼ So Delicious

Cookies

▼ Alpendough
▼ Eat Pastry
▼ Enjoy Life
▼ Just Cookie Dough
▼ Lenny & Larry's
▼ Oreo

Chocolate Chips

▼ Enjoy Life
▼ King David Kosher
▼ Trader Joe's Semi–Sweet Chocolate Chips

How the Chapters Work

If you're new to cooking, vegan or not, don't fret. This book is a choose-your-own-adventure sort of good time; the recipes you choose to make can be as simple or as involved as you want them to be. It's your adventure—choose wisely.

To get you acquainted with the book, start with the first chapter, "Basic Betty." There you'll find comfort-food favorites such as Easy Creamy Shells and Cheese (page 16); burgers, meatballs, or sausage patties in Meet the Meats (page 18); and Chocolate Chip Cookie Dough (page 33). Starting here will get you comfortable enough to move forward in the book, where even more epicness awaits!

In addition to chapter 1, chapters 2 and 3 also tackle basics such as sauces, dips, and breads. These recipes can be used alone or as part of other recipes elsewhere in the book. For example, the recipe for Philly Cheesesteaks in chapter 1 (page 20) calls for The Cheesiest Cheese Sauce from chapter 2 (page 44). You'll see it then goes further, with a Cheesesteak Baked Potato Bowl (page 147) and Cheesesteak Pizza (page 115) allowing you to have fun and use the Philly Cheesesteaks filling (page 20) in a myriad of ways. Don't let this intimidate you! The recipes are designed to be built on top of each other for optimal epicness.

Throughout, I offer cooking hacks to expedite or streamline your process to make tackling creations with several recipes as easy as possible. Just take it one step at a time and focus on the fun of creating delicious, over-the-top food for yourself, friends, and family.

What's even more epic? Recipes that require parts of other recipes is a fantastic and crafty way to use leftovers. For instance, if you make a whole pan of Easy Creamy Shells and Cheese (page 16) and you're left with half the pan after feeding the family, it's time to make some Mac and Cheese Pretzel Bites (page 76)! The possibilities are endless.

I encourage you to start with the recipes in this book as they're written, then get creative, play with your food, and add your own spin on them to create your own plate of Epic! When all is said and done, cooking is about joy. I can't stress this enough. I didn't write this book for busy people on the go, throwing together family meals in a pinch. If you want that, by all means, pick up my first book, *The Simply Vegan Cookbook*, and I got you covered! *Epic Vegan* is about being creative, going the extra mile, and playing with your food, period. Now, turn on some tunes, get cooking, and have some FUN!

"When all is said and done, cooking is about joy."

CHAPTER 1

BASIC BETTY:
FUNdamental Recipes

QUINOA BACON BITS

BACON! Even vegans are obsessed with it. Because I enjoy smoky flavors in my meals, I created these bacon bits particularly for the Loaded Baked Potato Soup on page 140, but you will find use for them in several other recipes in this book! I also like to have them on hand to sprinkle over salads, soups, or even in sandwiches.

- ▶ 1 cup (185 g) cooked quinoa
- ▶ 1 tablespoon (15 ml) soy sauce
- ▶ 1 tablespoon (15 ml) olive oil
- ▶ 2 teaspoons (10 g) ketchup
- ▶ 1 teaspoon smoked paprika
- ▶ ½ teaspoon sea salt
- ▶ ½ teaspoon black pepper

In a medium bowl, mix together the quinoa, soy sauce, olive oil, ketchup, smoked paprika, salt, and pepper until well combined.

Heat a nonstick skillet over medium heat until it's hot. Add the quinoa mixture and spread in one layer. Cook 3 minutes, undisturbed (it will be hard to resist!). Using a spatula, scrape the quinoa off the bottom of the skillet, mix it around, and spread it in another single layer. Cook an additional 3 minutes.

Transfer the quinoa to a bowl, scraping the skillet to get any crispy stubborn bits off. Store cooled bacon bits in a sealed container in the refrigerator for up to 1 week.

Yield: 1 cup (160 g)

Tip

The quinoa will not necessarily crisp up when in the skillet; you might luck out and get some crispy pieces, but the purpose of this step is to dry out the quinoa a bit and release some of the robust flavors.

Create Your Epic

- ▶ Bacon Macaroni and Cheese BBQ Blue Burger (page 90)
- ▶ Stuffed-Crust Meatball Parm Pizza (page 112)
- ▶ Loaded Baked Potato Soup with Pretzel Bowls (page 140)
- ▶ I Try to Think About Elvis Ice Cream (page 171)

HEMP PARMESAN

In my first book, The Simply Vegan Cookbook, I made a walnut parmesan. In this book, I wanted to create a nut-free version that also packs a nutrient punch, so I turned to the good ole hemp seed. I like to have this condiment handy in the refrigerator to use on pizza and pasta at the ready!

- ▶ ½ cup (60 g) hemp seeds
- ▶ 2 tablespoons (10 g) nutritional yeast
- ▶ ½ teaspoon sea salt
- ▶ 1 teaspoon maple syrup

Add the hemp seeds, nutritional yeast, and salt to a high-speed blender or food processor. Blend on low speed for 30 seconds, scraping down the sides if needed. Add the maple syrup, ½ teaspoon at a time, pulsing the mixture until well combined. Store in a sealed container in the refrigerator for up to 1 week.

Yield: ½ cup (80 g)

Tip

You can use agave as a substitute if you don't have maple syrup on hand—or even organic cane sugar if you're really in a pinch.

Create Your Epic

- ▶ Pizzabon (page 108)
- ▶ Unicorn French Bread Pizza (page 118)

HAPPY HASH BROWNS

I love hash browns! You'll find a couple of recipes in this book that use them. One of my favorites is the Breakfast Platter Dog on page 94, but you can't go wrong pairing it with the Eggsellent Eggs on page 32 or the Breakfast Sausage Patties on page 18. Or maybe you'll just eat them by themselves. Whatever you do, be patient and let them cook up nice and crispy for maximum enjoyment! Fry or bake them—it's up to you.

- 3 medium russet potatoes (about 1½ pounds or 680 g), peeled and grated
- 1 small onion, grated
- ¼ cup (32 g) flax meal
- 1½ teaspoons dried rosemary
- ¾ teaspoon sea salt
- ½ teaspoon black pepper
- Canola oil or cooking spray

In a large bowl, combine the potatoes, onion, flax, rosemary, salt, and pepper until the potatoes are well coated. Let sit for 5 minutes, until the flax sticks to the potato mixture.

To fry the hash browns:
Line a plate with paper towels.

Heat ¼ inch (6 mm) of oil in a large skillet over medium heat. Using a ¼ cup measuring cup, scoop the potato mixture and shape into patties. Add to the skillet, and fry 2 to 4 minutes on each side, until browned and crispy. Transfer to the paper towel–lined plate.

Repeat with the remaining potato mixture, adding more oil to the skillet as needed.

To bake the hash browns:
Preheat the oven to 400°F (200°C, or gas mark 6). Line a baking sheet with parchment paper.

Using a ¼ cup measuring cup, scoop the potato mixture and shape into patties. Place on the prepared baking sheet and spritz lightly with cooking spray. Bake for 15 minutes, then remove from the oven. Flip the patties, lightly spritz with cooking spray, and bake for an additional 25 minutes, or until browned and crispy.

Yield: 8 to 10 patties

Tip

Spice it up! Hash browns can be so versatile. Get creative and add more spices like thyme or garlic, or even add vegetables such as red pepper and corn for a southwestern flair. Your hash brown is your canvas— play with it!

Create **Your** Epic

- Triple-Decker Brekky Sammy (page 88)
- Breakfast Platter Dog (page 94)

EASY CREAMY SHELLS AND CHEESE

This is my favorite mac and cheese I've created to date, and I love it baked or straight from the pot! I added the baked option because it reminds me of the frozen mac and cheese I had as a kid that came out of the oven with the crust around the edges. But really, I love it both ways!

- ▼ 1 batch The Cheesiest Cheese Sauce (page 44)
- ▼ 1 box (1 pound/454 g) medium shells pasta
- ▼ Hemp Parmesan (page 14, optional)

Prepare the pasta according to package directions and drain.

In the large pot that the shells were prepared in, combine the cheese sauce and the shells until the shells are entirely coated. Serve topped with the parmesan, if desired.

To bake: While the shells cook, preheat the oven to 400°F (200°C, or gas mark 6). Transfer the finished mac and cheese to a lightly greased 9 x 13-inch (23 x 33-cm) baking dish. Bake for 35 to 40 minutes, or until the edges have started to brown and crisp. Remove from the oven and sprinkle with the parmesan, if desired.

Yield: 8 servings

Tip

This recipe comes together in a cinch. While your pasta is cooking, whip up the cheese sauce. Crunch up potato chips for an extra-fun crust on top! Or go a step further and use the topping recipe from the Lobster Mac and Cheese on page 130.

Create Your Epic

- ▼ Mac and Cheese Pretzel Bites (page 76)
- ▼ Bacon Macaroni and Cheese BBQ Blue Burger (page 90)
- ▼ Lobster Mac and Cheese (page 130)

MEET THE MEATS

It's important for me to offer a multipurpose recipe for vegetable-grain meat in this book so you can make delicious burgers, sausage patties, and meatballs to have on hand, even if your local grocery store sells the latest in plant-based meats. This recipe is so versatile with just the switch of some spices. Also, if frying isn't your thing, I've included a general baking option.

For All-American Burgers:

- ▼ 2 tablespoons (30 ml) olive oil
- ▼ 1 cup (160 g) roughly chopped onion
- ▼ 1 cup (70 g) stemmed and chopped baby bella mushrooms
- ▼ 1 cup (125 g) crumbled tempeh
- ▼ 2 cloves garlic, minced
- ▼ 1 teaspoon allspice
- ▼ 1 teaspoon dried thyme
- ▼ ¾ cup (140 g) cooked brown rice
- ▼ ½ cup (50 g) vital wheat gluten (see Tip)
- ▼ ¼ cup (30 g) dried bread crumbs
- ▼ 2 tablespoons (28 ml) soy sauce
- ▼ 1 teaspoon sea salt
- ▼ ¼ teaspoon crushed red pepper flakes
- ▼ Canola oil or cooking spray

For Breakfast Sausage Patties:

- ▼ ½ teaspoon fennel seeds
- ▼ ½ teaspoon caraway seeds

For Meatballs:

- ▼ Omit allspice and thyme
- ▼ 2 cloves garlic, minced
- ▼ 2 teaspoons dried basil
- ▼ Canola oil or cooking spray

To make the burgers: Heat the olive oil in a large skillet over medium-high heat. Add the onion, mushrooms, and tempeh; sauté for 5 minutes, until soft. Add the garlic, allspice, and thyme, and cook 1 additional minute, until fragrant.

Add the brown rice, gluten, bread crumbs, soy sauce, salt, and crushed red pepper to a food processor. Add the onion-and-tempeh mixture, and process on low speed until a ball of dough is just starting to form; do not overprocess; there should still be some texture to the mixture. Let the mixture cool slightly, then form the mixture into a 4-inch-long (10-cm) log (see Tip). Cut the log crosswise into 4 patties (1 inch [2.5 cm] thick) and form to desired shape.

Slider option: If you wish to make sliders, cut each patty into 4 sections and re-form into 16 slider patties. Cook following the directions for the burgers.

Heat ¼ inch (6 mm) of canola oil in a large skillet over medium-high heat. Add 2 patties and fry 2 to 4 minutes on each side, or until browned and crispy. Repeat with the 2 remaining patties. Serve burgers topped as desired.

To make the sausages: Follow the directions for making the burgers, adding the fennel and caraway seeds with the other spices. Make a 6-inch-long (15-cm) log with the mixture. Slice the log crosswise into 8 patties (¾ inch [2 cm] thick). Fry or bake as desired, following the directions for the burger.

To make the meatballs: Follow the directions for making the burgers, omitting the allspice and thyme and adding the 2 additional cloves garlic and basil. Scoop a heaping tablespoon of the mixture and use your hands to form a meatball; you should end up with 16. To fry the meatballs, heat ¼ inch (6 mm) of canola oil in a large skillet over medium-high heat. Add the meatballs in 2 to 3 batches and fry for 4 to 6 minutes. Tilt the pan gently to rotate the balls during cooking to brown all sides. Use the general baking option instead, if desired.

Baking option: Preheat the oven to 350°F (175°C, or gas mark 4). Line a baking sheet with parchment paper. Place the prepared burgers, patties, or meatballs on the baking sheet and coat lightly with cooking spray. Bake for 15 minutes, and remove from the oven. Flip, spray again lightly with cooking spray, and bake an additional 15 to 20 minutes, or until browned and firm.

Yield: 4 burgers (or 16 sliders), 8 sausage patties, or 16 meatballs

Tip

If you don't have vital wheat gluten, don't stress; you can still make these meats delicious, though they won't be as firm or have the same chew. Just add ¼ to ½ cup (30 to 60 g) extra bread crumbs until you get a dough-like texture. To create the "log" for the burgers and sausage, transfer the mixture onto a surface and form it into a ball. Push it down on the surface and roll it back and forth with your palms flat, forming it into a log shape with smooth sides, until you reach the desired length.

Create Your Epic

▼ Triple-Decker Brekky Sammy (page 88)

▼ Bacon Macaroni and Cheese BBQ Blue Burger (page 90)

▼ Bacon–Cinnamon Roll Burger with Peanut Butter (page 92)

▼ The Hangover Breakfast Sandwich (page 102)

▼ Mac Daddy Crunch Burrito (page 103)

▼ Stuffed-Crust Meatball Parm Pizza (page 112)

PHILLY CHEESESTEAKS

There are five foods that every vegan business across the United States claims to be the best at making: macaroni and cheese, pizza, the Reuben sandwich, nachos, and the Philly cheesesteak sandwich. While filming *The Vegan Roadie*, I tasted many of these items from several different chefs. I give a tie for the best cheesesteak to Blackbird Pizzeria and Wiz Kid in Philadelphia, both featured in episodes of *The Vegan Roadie*. This recipe is dedicated to the City of Brotherly Love and Sisterly Affection.

- 2 tablespoons (30 ml) olive oil, divided
- 1 white onion, sliced
- 1 green bell pepper, sliced
- 2 vegan Italian sausages, halved crosswise, then thinly sliced lengthwise
- 2 large portobello mushroom caps, stemmed and thinly sliced
- 1 tablespoon (15 ml) soy sauce
- ½ teaspoon black pepper
- ¼ teaspoon sea salt
- 4 to 6 vegan hoagie rolls
- About 1 cup (235 ml) The Cheesiest Cheese Sauce (page 44)

Heat 1 tablespoon (15 ml) of the olive oil in a large skillet over medium-high heat. Add the onion and bell pepper. Sauté for 4 to 6 minutes, until soft and starting to char. Remove from the skillet and set aside.

In the same skillet, heat the remaining 1 tablespoon (15 ml) oil. Add the sausages and mushrooms. Sauté for 4 to 6 minutes, or until the mushrooms have wilted and the sausage has browned. Add the pepper-onion mixture back to the skillet along with the soy sauce, black pepper, and salt. Stir until everything is well combined.

Divide the mixture evenly among the hoagie rolls, and top with a generous amount of the cheese sauce. Serve hot.

Yield: 4 to 6 sandwiches

Tip

Don't want to add the processed sausage? No sweat! Add thin strips of tempeh (about ½ block) or 2 more thinly sliced portobello caps to the mix instead.

Create **Your** Epic

- Cheesesteak Baked Potato Bowl (page 147)

SIMPLY SEITAN

Seitan is one of those versatile items that people seem to be terrified of making. But once you make it, you will come back to it again and again! While you easily can get it in some stores these days, don't be shy—play around with this recipe and see for yourself just how easy it is to make.

- 1½ cups (150 g) vital wheat gluten

- 2 tablespoons (10 g) nutritional yeast

- 1 teaspoon poultry seasoning

- 1 cup (235 ml) water

- 2 tablespoons (30 g) ketchup

- Juice of ½ lemon

- 4 cups (940 ml) vegetable broth

- ¼ cup (60 ml) soy sauce

- 3 cloves garlic, halved

In a large bowl, whisk together the gluten, nutritional yeast, and poultry seasoning.

In a separate bowl, whisk together the water, ketchup, and lemon juice until well combined.

Add the wet mixture to the dry, and mix together with a fork until well combined. Knead with your hands for about 4 minutes, until a thick elastic dough forms.

In a large saucepan or pot, combine the broth, soy sauce, and garlic. Bring to a boil. Cut the dough in half and place both halves in the saucepan. Return to a boil, then reduce to a simmer. Partially cover the pot so that the lid allows steam to escape, and simmer for 30 minutes. Rotate the pieces of dough, flipping them over. Partially cover and simmer for an additional 30 minutes. Uncover, remove from the heat, and let the dough cool completely in the broth.

Seitan can be stored in the broth, covered, and kept in the refrigerator for up to 10 days. It can also be stored in a sealed container (with the broth) in the freezer for up to 6 months. Thaw overnight in the refrigerator.

Yield: 12 servings

Tip

Rather than kneading by hand, you can absolutely make this in a stand mixer with the dough hook if you have one available to you. Knead for 2 to 4 minutes on medium speed, or until an elastic dough forms.

Create Your Epic

- Fried Chicken (page 23)
- Almost Famous Buffalo Chicken Lasagna (page 126)

FRIED CHICKEN

I know, so much fried stuff, right? But don't worry. As with most fried offerings in this book, this recipe also offers a baked option. If you're searching for that finger-lickin'-good blast from the past, look no further. My favorite epic recipe to use this fried chicken in is the Fried Chicken 'n Waffle Benedict Sandwich on page 99, paired with the Hollandaise for Days on page 40—it's a winning combo! Sometimes I serve it with the Buffalo Sauce from the Everything Buffalo Cauliflower Bites on page 84 on the side if I'm feeling spicy!

- ▼ 1 cup (235 ml) unsweetened soy or almond milk
- ▼ 1 tablespoon (15 ml) apple cider vinegar
- ▼ 1 cup (125 g) all-purpose flour
- ▼ 1 tablespoon (7 g) paprika
- ▼ 1½ teaspoons sea salt
- ▼ 1 teaspoon dried oregano
- ▼ 1 teaspoon dried parsley
- ▼ ½ teaspoon dried thyme
- ▼ ½ teaspoon onion powder
- ▼ ½ teaspoon garlic powder
- ▼ ½ teaspoon black pepper
- ▼ 1 batch Simply Seitan (page 22), pieces torn or cut to desired size and shape (see Tip)
- ▼ Canola oil or cooking spray

In a small bowl, combine the milk and vinegar. Let sit for 5 minutes, until thickened.

In a shallow bowl, whisk together the flour, paprika, salt, oregano, parsley, thyme, onion powder, garlic powder, and pepper.

Submerge the pieces of seitan in the milk mixture and then dredge through the flour mixture until coated on all sides. Shake off the excess and set aside. Continue with the remaining seitan.

To fry the chicken: In a wok or large saucepan, pour 3 inches (7.5 cm) of canola oil. Heat to 350°F (175°C) when tested with a candy thermometer or until bubbles form around the handle of a wooden spoon when inserted into the oil. Line a plate with paper towels.

Carefully transfer pieces of seitan to the oil, 2 or 3 pieces at a time, and fry for 2 minutes, or until browned and crispy. Remove from the oil with a slotted spoon and transfer to the paper towel–lined plate. Repeat with the remaining seitan.

To bake the chicken: Preheat the oven to 425°F (220°C, or gas mark 7). Line a baking sheet with parchment paper.

Set the pieces of coated seitan on the prepared baking sheet. Spray the tops of each piece lightly with cooking spray, and bake for 15 minutes. Remove from the oven, spray again until light brown, flip, spray lightly again with cooking spray, and bake for an additional 15 minutes, until darker in color and crunchy. If the side flipped up is still light in color, spray with a little more cooking spray until darker.

Yield: 6 to 8 servings

Tip

You can tear the seitan apart with your hands to get that rustic nonuniform look, or use kitchen shears or a knife to cut pieces in uniform size—it's your call! And by all means, make what YOU want. Chicken nuggets? Cut into nugget sizes, then dredge and fry 'em! Popcorn chicken? Chicken strips? Chicken cutlets? You know what to do.

Create **Your** Epic

- ▼ Creamy Jambalaya Pasta with Crispy Chicken (page 123)
- ▼ Fried Chicken Noodle Soup (page 138)

LOBSTER ROLLS

I can't say I ever had a particular liking for lobster rolls when I wasn't vegan, but I did have them on a few trips to Maine. But now that I've created this lobster roll recipe, I haven't been able to stop making them! I love to pull these out for summer gatherings.

- ▼ 1 can (14 ounces/396 g) artichoke hearts, drained and roughly chopped

- ▼ 1 can (14 ounces/396 g) hearts of palm, drained and roughly chopped

- ▼ 2 ribs celery, halved and thinly sliced

- ▼ ½ cup (90 g) roughly chopped roasted red pepper

- ▼ ½ cup (115 g) vegan mayonnaise

- ▼ ¼ cup (40 g) minced red onion

- ▼ 1 tablespoon (15 ml) canola oil

- ▼ Juice of ½ lemon

- ▼ 1 tablespoon (4 g) dulse flakes

- ▼ 2 teaspoons (5 g) Old Bay Seasoning

- ▼ ¼ teaspoon sea salt

- ▼ ¼ teaspoon black pepper

- ▼ 4 vegan sandwich rolls

In a medium bowl, combine the artichokes, hearts of palm, celery, red pepper, mayonnaise, onion, canola oil, lemon juice, dulse, Old Bay, salt, and black pepper until well mixed. Use immediately or refrigerate for 8 hours or up to overnight to really let the flavors marinate. I highly recommend the overnight option if time allows.

Divide the mixture among the 4 sandwich rolls.

Yield: 4 servings

Tip

Go the extra mile and use some vegan butter to toast the sandwich rolls before piling on the lobster filling. For a how-to on toasting your buns, see the Tip on page 94.

Create Your Epic

- ▼ Lobster Roll 'n a Biscuit Sliders (page 92)

- ▼ Lobster Mac and Cheese (page 130)

MOM'S CHILI

My mom was the chili and goulash queen when I was a kid. In the fall, there wasn't a night during the week when we didn't have one or the other for dinner, and I loved the smell of them cooking! So this is my mother's recipe, straightforward and simple, veganized. Thanks to the delicious vegan meats on the market these days, I've served this to my mother, and she hasn't even noticed the difference! I love to serve it with vegan cheddar shreds, Avocado Sour Cream (page 50), and sliced scallions on top.

- ▶ 2 tablespoons (30 ml) olive oil
- ▶ 2 ribs celery, chopped
- ▶ 1 onion, chopped
- ▶ ½ green bell pepper, chopped
- ▶ 1 bag (10 to 13 ounces, or 280 to 369 g) frozen vegan beef crumbles
- ▶ 2 cloves garlic, chopped
- ▶ 2 cans (15.5 ounces/439 g) kidney beans, drained and rinsed
- ▶ 1 can (28 ounces/794 g) diced tomatoes
- ▶ 1 can (15 ounces/425 g) tomato sauce
- ▶ 1 tablespoon (8 g) chili powder
- ▶ 2 teaspoons (5 g) ground cumin
- ▶ 1 teaspoon sea salt
- ▶ ½ teaspoon black pepper

Heat the oil in a stockpot over medium heat. Add the celery, onion, and bell pepper. Sauté for 3 to 5 minutes, or until softened. Add the beef crumbles; sauté 5 to 8 minutes, or until broken down and slightly browned. Add the garlic and sauté 1 additional minute, until fragrant.

Add the beans, tomatoes with their juice, tomato sauce, chili powder, cumin, salt, and black pepper. Stir until well combined. Bring to a simmer, cover, and cook for 35 minutes, until the flavors blend together. Taste and adjust seasoning as desired.

Yield: 8 servings (2½ quarts)

Tip

This chili freezes really well. Scoop cooled leftovers into freezer bags, label, and stick in the freezer for super-easy meals or even to put on top of nachos.

Not feeling vegan beef crumbles? Veg it up! Add 2 cups (10 ounces/340 g) of 1-inch (2.5-cm) diced butternut squash or sugar pumpkin for a winter squash chili.

Create Your Epic

- ▶ Chili Cheese Potato Wedges with Quinoa Bacon Bits (page 77)
- ▶ Bless-Your-Heart Bowl (page 146)

CRISPY DRIVE-THRU POTATO WEDGES

We all know that we can cut up a potato, toss it with some oil, and bake it in the oven to get easy and delicious at-home "french fries." But let's kick it up a notch. Some fast food restaurants serve fries that are superior to others, and this recipe is a replica of one of my personal favorites from my nonvegan days, KFC. The good news is you don't have to fry them to get those robust flavors; I offer both fried and baked options with this recipe, so pick your pleasure.

For Frying:

- 1 cup (235 ml) unsweetened soy or almond milk
- 1 tablespoon (15 ml) apple cider vinegar
- Canola oil
- 1 cup (125 g) all-purpose flour
- 1 teaspoon black pepper
- ½ teaspoon sea salt
- ¼ teaspoon paprika
- ¼ teaspoon garlic powder
- 2 large russet potatoes, each potato cut into 16 vertical wedges
- Freshly chopped herbs and additional spices, for sprinkling (optional)

For Baking:

- 2 large russet potatoes, each potato cut into 16 vertical wedges
- 1 tablespoon (15 ml) olive oil
- ½ teaspoon Old Bay Seasoning
- ½ teaspoon garlic powder
- ¼ tablespoon (4 g) sea salt
- ¼ teaspoon black pepper

To fry the wedges: In a small bowl, combine the milk and vinegar, and let sit 5 minutes, until thickened.

In a wok or large saucepan, pour 3 inches (8 cm) of canola oil. Heat the oil to 350°F (175°C) when tested with a candy thermometer, or until bubbles form around the handle of a wooden spoon when inserted into the oil. Line a plate with paper towels.

In a shallow bowl, combine the flour, pepper, salt, paprika, and garlic powder.

In small batches, submerge the wedges in the milk mixture, allowing excess to drip off. Dredge in the flour mixture until completely coated.

Use tongs to carefully transfer the coated wedges, 6 to 8 at a time, to the oil and fry for 5 minutes, or until browned and crispy. Use a slotted spoon to transfer the wedges to the paper towel–lined plate. Repeat with the remaining wedges.

While the wedges are still hot, sprinkle with your favorite chopped fresh herbs, such as parsley, rosemary, thyme, or even some chives (if desired). Season it up with some flaked or truffle salt,

freshly ground black pepper, or more Old Bay. The fries are your canvas; create with flavors you love.

To bake the wedges: Preheat the oven to 475°F (246°C, or gas mark 9). Line a baking sheet with parchment paper.

In a large bowl, toss the potato wedges with the olive oil until well coated.

In a small bowl, mix together the Old Bay, garlic powder, salt, and pepper. Sprinkle half of the seasoning mixture over the potatoes and toss well to coat. Sprinkle the remaining seasoning on the potatoes and toss again until well coated.

Transfer the wedges to the prepared baking sheet and bake for 12 minutes. Flip and bake an additional 10 to 12 minutes, or until browned and crispy.

Yield: 2 servings

Tip

If you find you didn't get the crispiness you desired when baking, set your oven to broil after the wedges have baked. Broil for 2 minutes, or until desired crispiness is reached. Everyone's broiler differs in intensity; be sure to keep a close eye so you don't burn your wedges!

Create Your Epic

- Chili Cheese Potato Wedges with Quinoa Bacon Bits (page 77)
- Jumbo Phish 'n Chips Sushi Roll (page 82)

MURPHY'S SLAW

People get very serious about their coleslaw, so serious that while working an event a few years ago and tasked with making the coleslaw, I politely declined. I don't take it so seriously; I think slaw should be easy and come together in a flash. So that's what I give you here; if you feel differently, feel free to embellish this recipe with unicorn sparkles and pickle juice found only in a rare seasonal dill pickle from the Amazon rainforest (or whatever ingredient you simply feel coleslaw can't be without).

- ▶ 2 cups (140 g) shredded red cabbage
- ▶ 2 cups (220 g) shredded carrots
- ▶ ¼ cup (60 g) vegan mayonnaise
- ▶ Juice of ½ lemon
- ▶ 1 tablespoon (20 g) maple syrup
- ▶ ½ teaspoon sea salt
- ▶ ½ teaspoon black pepper

In a large bowl, mix together the cabbage, carrots, mayonnaise, lemon juice, syrup, salt, and pepper until well combined.

Yield: 4 servings (4 cups/420 g)

Tip

Buy preshredded carrots and cabbage to save time! I will not judge you for this; I will give you a standing ovation. I use red cabbage because I love the color, but feel free to use the cabbage that you like best.

Create **Your** Epic

- ▶ Hushpuppy Phish Fillet Sandwich (page 100)

BEER-BATTERED TOFU PHISH

When my husband, David, and I were in London on a quick trip, we heard of a pub with vegan fish and chips. After much back and forth and getting the timing correct on when there was dinner service, we finally ordered the plate with delight ... to huge disappointment. I took to re-creating a version on my own, making dozens of attempts before settling on this one, which uses a sheet of nori. Never underestimate the power of nori—it's completely satisfying.

- ▼ 1 block (14 ounces/396 g) extra-firm tofu
- ▼ 1¼ cups (157 g) all-purpose flour, divided
- ▼ 1 cup (140 g) stone-ground cornmeal or polenta
- ▼ ¼ cup (32 g) cornstarch
- ▼ 1 tablespoon (8 g) Old Bay Seasoning
- ▼ 1 teaspoon sea salt
- ▼ 1½ cups (355 ml) vegan lager-style beer
- ▼ Juice of 1 lemon
- ▼ Canola oil
- ▼ 3 sheets nori, quartered

Cut the tofu lengthwise into three sheets. Cut the sheets widthwise across the block into 4 strips to create 12 pieces total.

In a medium bowl, whisk together 1 cup (125 g) of the flour, the cornmeal, cornstarch, Old Bay, and salt. Slowly add the beer, then add the lemon juice and whisk well until a thick batter forms.

Spread the remaining ¼ cup (32 g) flour on a plate.

In a wok or large saucepan, pour 3 inches (8 cm) of canola oil. Heat the oil to 350°F (175°C) when tested with a candy thermometer, or until bubbles form around the handle of a wooden spoon when inserted into the oil. Line a plate with paper towels.

Wrap each piece of tofu in a quarter piece of nori. Press the nori to the tofu until the moisture makes it stick. Dredge the nori-covered tofu in flour, then dunk into the bowl of batter, submerging completely.

Use a fork to gently transfer the tofu to the frying oil. Fry for 2 to 3 minutes, until golden brown. Use a slotted spoon to transfer the tofu to the paper towel–lined plate. Continue with the remaining tofu.

Serve with a side of Crispy Drive-Thru Potato Wedges (page 26) and Murphy's Slaw (page 27) for a traditional plate of fish and chips, or use in recipes as directed.

Yield: 3 or 4 servings

Tip

Don't overcrowd the pot or wok; frying 2 at a time is best. If necessary, reheat leftovers by baking in a 300°F (149°C, or gas mark 2) oven for 10 minutes.

Create **Your** Epic

- ▼ Jumbo Phish 'n Chips Sushi Roll (page 82)
- ▼ Hushpuppy Phish Fillet Sandwich (page 100)

Use basic recipes from this chapter to "Create Your Epic" in chapters to come. Hushpuppy Fish Fillet Sandwich, Pizzabons, Pretzel Bites, Fried Chicken Strips, Franks 'n Mac Pizza, Noritos Los Tacos, Caramel-Stuffed Cookies 'n Cream Cupcakes, Fudgy AF Brownies, Chocolate Chip Cookies, Soft Pretzels, Birthday Cake, Epic PB&J Bars, and Sweet Chili Cocktail Peanuts.

CRAB RANGOON

When I was a kid in Michigan, ordering crab rangoon was a staple for the table when we went out for Chinese food. When I moved to NYC, I remember being so disappointed to discover this was not a typical item on Chinese menus. Needless to say, it was my mission to re-create these for very personal reasons. Hearts of palm give it the texture usually provided by the crab, but let's face it, it's that luscious cream cheese with the crunchy wonton everyone loves! Speaking of cream cheese, these were tested several times with various brands, and the tofu-based cream cheeses complement it best, with the nut-based cream cheeses coming in second; the Dreamy Creamy Cream Cheese on page 41 will also successfully take you to the finish line.

- ½ cup Dreamy Creamy Cream Cheese (page 41) or store-bought tofu-based cream cheese
- 1 tablespoon (15 ml) water from the can of hearts of palm
- 1 teaspoon lemon juice
- ¾ teaspoon Old Bay Seasoning
- 1 pinch sea salt
- 2 tablespoons (18 g) minced hearts of palm
- 16 vegan wonton or dumpling wrappers
- Canola oil
- Sweet Thai Chili Sauce (page 46), for dipping (optional)

In a medium bowl, mix together the cream cheese, hearts of palm water, lemon juice, Old Bay, and salt until well combined. Stir in the hearts of palm until evenly dispersed.

Prepare a small bowl with water for sealing the edges of the wontons.

Set a wonton wrapper on a work surface. Scoop 1 heaping teaspoon of the cream cheese mixture into the center of the wrapper. Create a basic triangle wonton or get epic with a "parcel" fold, as pictured (see Tip).

To make triangle rangoons: Moisten the edges of the wonton with a wet fingertip, then fold it in half over the filling to create a triangle, carefully pressing out excess air before you press down and seal the wonton— be sure to seal the edges tightly to avoid the filling from falling out. Set aside on parchment paper as you work through them so the bottoms don't stick to the work surface.

To make "parcel" fold rangoons: Moisten the edges of the wonton with a wet fingertip. Lift and press two opposing corners of the wonton together in the center over the filling. Lift the remaining two opposing corners to the middle and press all corners together, forming a small parcel. Gently press the edges of the seams together to form a solid seal. Be careful not to allow any air to remain inside as you seal them. Set aside on parchment.

In a wok or large saucepan, pour 3 inches (8 cm) of canola oil. Heat the oil to 350°F (175°C), or until a small piece of wonton crisps up within seconds when set in the oil. Line a plate with paper towels.

Carefully transfer 2 or 3 wontons to the oil and fry for 1 to 2 minutes, or until golden brown. Remove with a slotted spoon and transfer to the paper towel–lined plate. Repeat with the remaining rangoons.

Serve with Sweet Thai Chili Sauce, if desired.

Yield: 16 rangoons

Tip

Can't wrap your brain around creating the "parcel" fold for the crab rangoon? This is what YouTube is made for! Find a YouTube tutorial and you'll be an expert in no time! If you're working with a round dumpling wrapper, you can achieve the same results; you'll just be folding in the four sides of the round to the center for the parcel, and the triangle shape will be a half moon— either will be delicious!

Create Your Epic

- Crab Rangoon Pizza (page 116)

EGGSELLENT EGGS

While companies are advancing in the world of vegan egg possibilities, I have yet to meet a replacement that totally hits the mark and doesn't break the bank. Tofu has always done the trick for me personally; seasoned just right, you can't go wrong. Use the same mix of spices here for either baked pieces of tofu egg or a fluffy scramble.

For Baked Tofu:

▼ 1 block (14 ounces/396 g) extra-firm tofu

▼ 2 tablespoons (30 ml) olive oil

▼ ½ teaspoon sea salt

▼ ½ teaspoon garlic powder

▼ ½ teaspoon onion powder

▼ ½ teaspoon ground turmeric

▼ ½ teaspoon Himalayan black salt (kala namak, optional)

▼ ¼ teaspoon black pepper

▼ ¼ teaspoon smoked paprika

For Scramble:

▼ ¼ cup (60 ml) vegetable broth

▼ 1 tablespoon (15 ml) olive oil

▼ Vegan meats and chopped fresh vegetables of choice (see Tip)

To make the baked tofu:
Preheat the oven to 425°F (220°C, or gas mark 7). Line a baking sheet with parchment paper.

Cut the tofu into 3 sheets lengthwise, then cut each sheet into 4 squares to create 12 pieces. Set the tofu pieces on the prepared baking sheet.

In a small bowl, whisk together the olive oil, sea salt, garlic powder, onion powder, turmeric, black salt (if using), pepper, and smoked paprika.

Using a pastry brush, brush the tops of each tofu piece with the mixture. Bake for 12 minutes, and remove from the oven. Flip the tofu, brush with the remaining seasoning mixture, and bake for an additional 12 minutes, or until bright yellow and sizzling.

To make the scrambled tofu: Quarter the block of tofu, and add 1 piece to a high-speed blender; set aside the other 3 pieces.

Add the vegetable broth to the blender, along with the olive oil, sea salt, garlic powder, onion powder, turmeric, black salt (if using), pepper, and paprika. Blend until smooth and creamy.

Heat the oil in a large skillet over medium heat. If using the scramble in another recipe, skip to the next step. Sauté vegan meats and vegetables for your scramble (see Tip).

Crumble the remaining 3 pieces of tofu into the skillet, stirring until the tofu is well combined with meats and veggies, if using. Add the mixture from the blender and stir until everything is coated. Bring to a simmer and cook for 4 to 6 minutes, or until the liquid thickens and the mixture becomes a little dryer. Serve hot.

Yield: 4 servings

Tip

Sauté vegan meats and vegetables for your scramble until the meats are slightly browned and the vegetables are tender—3 to 5 minutes should do the trick, depending on your meat and veggie choices. My favorites add-ins are sausage, red peppers, and spinach!

Create **Your Epic**

▼ Breakfast Nachos (page 78)

▼ Triple-Decker Brekky Sammy (page 88)

▼ Breakfast Platter Dog (page 94)

▼ The Hangover Breakfast Sandwich (page 102)

▼ Deep-Dish Brunch Pizza (page 106)

▼ Savory Cheddar Fondue Waffle Bowl (page 139)

CHOCOLATE CHIP COOKIE DOUGH

Anything with the words "cookie dough" in the title always catches my attention. Cookie dough ice cream, cookie dough cake, and cookie dough truffles … you name it, I'll eat it. You can enjoy this recipe in raw cookie dough form or bake cookies to take to any gathering, or both! You'll also find a few recipes later in the book that use both the raw and baked versions; go for the gold with the Double-Stacked Cookie Dough Cake on page 168 to delight a cookie-dough lover on their birthday, for the win!

- 1 cup (225 g) vegan butter, room temperature
- ¾ cup (150 g) organic cane sugar
- ¾ cup (170 g) packed organic light brown sugar
- ¼ cup (60 g) unsweetened applesauce
- 1 teaspoon vanilla extract
- 2¼ cups (282 g) all-purpose flour
- 1 teaspoon sea salt
- 1 teaspoon baking soda
- 1½ cups (175 g, or one 10-ounce bag) vegan mini or regular chocolate chips

To make the cookie dough:

In a large bowl with a hand mixer, or in a stand mixer with the paddle attachment, cream together the butter, cane sugar, and brown sugar at medium speed until smooth and light, about 2 minutes. Beat in the applesauce and vanilla until combined.

Add the flour, salt, and baking soda. Mix until a dough forms. Fold in the chocolate chips and mix until evenly dispersed throughout.

Eat the dough as is or chill in the freezer for 30 minutes before baking or using in recipes.

To bake as cookies: Preheat the oven to 375°F (190°C, or gas mark 5). Line 2 baking sheets with parchment paper.

Scoop rounded tablespoons of cookie dough onto the prepared baking sheets, leaving 2 inches (5 cm) between each cookie. Bake for 9 to 11 minutes, or until just starting to brown. Remove from the oven and cool for 10 minutes.

Yield: 4 cups (1,100 g) raw cookie dough or about 3 dozen baked cookies

Tip

Make the cookie dough ahead and freeze for up to 1 month; thaw at room temperature for 2 hours before use. Or keep it in a sealed container in the refrigerator for up to 1 week and bake cookies when the craving strikes. This will take the place of that tube of processed cookie dough in your fridge!

Create **Your** Epic

- Cookie Dough Frostee (page 162)
- Double-Stacked Cookie Dough Cake (page 168)
- S'mores Cookie Cups (page 174)

CAKE BATTER AND BUTTERCREAM FROSTING

Cake! Cake to me means celebrations and friends, and also "the morning after"—I love a piece of birthday cake for breakfast the morning after my birthday! I hope this vanilla cake makes its way into many celebrations in your life, no matter what form it takes in the varied recipes in this book (some use the cake, some use the batter). For an extra bonus, turn this recipe into cupcakes or carrot cake with just a few added ingredients.

For Cake Batter:

▼ Canola oil or cooking spray

▼ 3 cups (375 g) all-purpose flour

▼ 2 cups (400 g) organic cane sugar

▼ 2 teaspoons (10 g) baking soda

▼ 1 teaspoon sea salt

▼ 2 cups (475 ml) unsweetened soy or almond milk

▼ ¾ cup (177 ml) canola oil

▼ 2 tablespoons (28 ml) vanilla extract

▼ 2 tablespoons (28 ml) apple cider vinegar

For Buttercream Frosting:

▼ ½ cup (112 g) vegan butter, room temperature

▼ ½ cup (50 g) nonhydrogenated vegetable shortening, room temperature

▼ 1½ teaspoons vanilla extract

▼ 3½ cups (420 g) organic confectioners' sugar

▼ 1 to 3 teaspoons (5 to 15 ml) unsweetened soy or almond milk (as needed)

To make the cake: Preheat the oven to 350°F (175°C, or gas mark 4). Lightly coat 2 round 9-inch (23-cm) cake pans with canola oil or cooking spray. Line with parchment paper (see Tip).

In a large bowl, whisk together the flour, sugar, baking soda, and salt. Add the milk, canola oil, vanilla, and vinegar. Mix until well incorporated.

Divide the batter evenly into each prepared cake pan. Bake for 30 to 35 minutes, or until a toothpick inserted into the middle comes out clean.

Let the cakes cool completely before removing from the pans. Before frosting, peel off the parchment and cut off the domes of each cake to create flat tops.

To make the buttercream frosting: In a large bowl with a hand mixer, or in a stand mixer with the paddle attachment, cream together the butter, shortening, and vanilla, starting on low speed and increasing to medium. Beat until smooth.

Set the mixer back to low speed. Add the confectioners' sugar, 1 cup at a time, until the sugar is just mixed in. Increase to medium speed and beat until fluffy, 2 to 3 minutes. If the buttercream is a little too thick, add milk by the teaspoon until the desired consistency is reached. Set aside at room temperature until the cakes are ready to be frosted, then frost as desired.

Cupcake variation: Line a cupcake tin with cupcake liners and fill each ¾ full with batter. Bake at 350°F (175°C, or gas mark 4) for 18 to 22 minutes, or until a toothpick inserted into the middle of one comes out clean. Allow to cool before frosting as desired.

Carrot cake variation: To the vanilla cake batter's dry ingredients, add ½ cup (75 g) dark brown sugar, 2 teaspoons pumpkin pie spice, and 1 teaspoon ground cinnamon. After the wet ingredients have been mixed in, stir in 2 cups (220 g) shredded carrots, 1 cup (120 g) crushed walnuts, and 1 cup (145 g) golden raisins until well distributed. Bake as the vanilla cake, cool, and frost. Replace the shortening in the frosting with vegan cream cheese for a traditional cream cheese frosting.

Yield: 12 cake slices or 24 cupcakes

Tip

Cut a piece of parchment paper to size by placing the round pan on the paper, tracing around it with a pencil, and cutting it out; it should fit perfectly in the pan. Want sprinkles on the side of that cake? See the sprinkles tip in the Birthday Cake Shake recipe on page 156. Or top the cake with fresh berries or organic edible flowers for something extra special.

Create Your Epic

▼ Cinnamon French Toast Shake (page 154)

▼ Birthday Cake Shake (page 156)

▼ Strawberry Short Shake (page 158)

▼ Pumpkin Cream Cheese Latte Shake (page 160)

▼ Caramel-Stuffed Cookies 'n Cream Cupcakes (page 167)

▼ Double-Stacked Cookie Dough Cake (page 168)

FUDGY AF BROWNIES

Brownies have always and forever been one of the easiest baked goods to whip up when you have guests coming over and you want to have a sweet treat to offer. These beauties are no exception; with the addition of chocolate chips they become nice and fudgy too! Add tofu- or nut-based vegan cream cheese for a luscious creamy swirl bonus (see Tip).

- Cooking spray
- 2 tablespoons (28 ml) water
- 1 tablespoon (7 g) flax meal
- 2 cups (250 g) all-purpose flour
- 2 cups (400 g) organic cane sugar
- ¾ cup (65 g) unsweetened cocoa powder
- 1 teaspoon baking soda
- 1 teaspoon sea salt
- ¾ cup (177 ml) canola oil
- ½ cup (120 ml) unsweetened soy or almond milk
- 1 tablespoon (15 ml) vanilla extract
- 1½ cups (175 g) vegan chocolate chips or chunks

Preheat the oven to 350°F (175°C, or gas mark 4). Line a 9 x 9-inch (23 x 23-cm) baking dish with parchment paper and lightly coat it with cooking spray.

Combine the water and flax in a small bowl. Whisk well, and set aside for 5 minutes to thicken.

In a large bowl, whisk together the flour, sugar, cocoa powder, baking soda, and salt. Add the canola oil, milk, vanilla, and flax mixture. Mix together with a wooden spoon until well combined. Fold in the chocolate chips until evenly distributed. Transfer to the prepared baking dish, spreading the batter evenly to fill the dish.

Bake for 35 to 40 minutes, or until the top looks dry and a toothpick inserted into the center comes out without batter sticking to it. Let cool completely in the pan before cutting. To speed up the cooling process, see the Tip on page 185.

Cut into 9 squares for large brownies and 12 for smaller. Store in a sealed container or wrap in plastic wrap and keep at room temperature for 3 days, or store in the freezer for up to 3 months.

Yield: 9 or 12 servings

Tip

Add 4 to 6 dollops of softened vegan cream cheese to the top of the brownies before you bake them. Swirl the dollops into the batter with a butter knife, bake as directed, and the cream cheese will brown a little when they are ready.

Create Your Epic

- Ultimate Caramel Cookie Brownie Shake (page 152)
- Power Tower Brownie Sundae (page 178)

VERY VANILLA ICE CREAM

What I love most about vanilla ice cream is that it creates a great base for other ice creams to take shape! It's not written in stone in this book, but I would try this ice cream with bits of Chocolate Chip Cookie Dough (page 33) crumbled in or with some of the Silky Sunflower Caramel Sauce (page 52) swirled in. Really, the options are endless; get creative and have fun with it!

- ▶ 1 cup (137 g) raw cashews, soaked in water overnight or boiled for 10 minutes and drained
- ▶ 1 can (13.5 ounces/983 ml) full-fat unsweetened coconut milk
- ▶ ¾ cup (175 ml) water
- ▶ ½ cup (100 g) organic cane sugar
- ▶ 1 tablespoon (15 ml) vanilla extract
- ▶ ¼ teaspoon sea salt
- ▶ 1 tablespoon (15 ml) vodka (optional)

Freeze the ice cream maker base according to the manufacturer's instructions; for most brands, it's overnight before making the ice cream.

In a high-speed blender, combine the cashews, coconut milk, water, sugar, vanilla, salt, and vodka (if using). Blend until smooth and creamy. Transfer to a bowl with a lid and refrigerate for 3 hours, or until cooled all the way through.

Transfer the mixture to the ice cream maker and prepare according to the manufacturer's instructions.

Transfer to a sealed container and freeze overnight. Homemade ice cream should be enjoyed ASAP but will last for up to 2 weeks!

Yield: about 1 quart (750 g)

Tip

The vodka helps reduce the chance of the ice cream being icy, promoting a creamier consistency, but it's not absolutely necessary. Before sealing the finished container, you can also press plastic wrap directly onto the ice cream to push out as much air as possible to help eliminate crystallization.

Create **Your** Epic

- ▶ Most of the recipes in chapter 9 (page 150)
- ▶ I Try to Think About Elvis Ice Cream (page 171)
- ▶ Sneaky Pickle Pineapple Ice Cream (page 175)
- ▶ Kale Me Crazy Ice Cream (page 177)
- ▶ Power Tower Brownie Sundae (page 178)
- ▶ The Hotel Cookie Ice Cream Sandwich (page 184)

CHAPTER 2

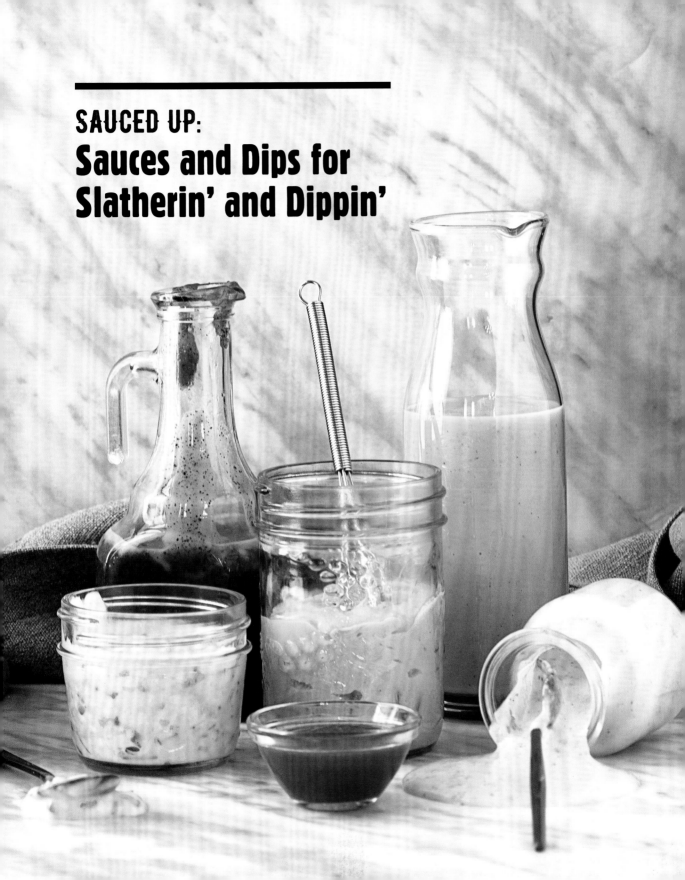

SAUCED UP:
Sauces and Dips for Slatherin' and Dippin'

BEET MARINARA

After the beet ketchup craze, I couldn't resist creating a beet marinara. This sauce really makes the Unicorn French Bread Pizza on page 118 pop, but it's also delicious for any pasta dish, pizza base, or dipping sauce.

- 2 tablespoons (28 ml) olive oil
- 1 onion, chopped
- 4 cloves garlic, minced
- 1 can (28 ounces/794 g) crushed tomatoes
- 1 cup (225 g) peeled and diced beets
- 1 tablespoon (3 g) dried oregano
- 1 teaspoon dried basil
- 1 teaspoon sea salt
- ¼ teaspoon crushed red pepper flakes
- ¼ cup (80 g) maple syrup

Heat the oil in a large skillet over medium heat. Add the onion and sauté for 3 to 5 minutes, until softened. Add the garlic and sauté an additional 1 minute, until fragrant.

Add the tomatoes, beets, oregano, basil, salt, and crushed red pepper. Stir until well combined, cover, and simmer, reducing heat if necessary, for 20 minutes.

Carefully transfer the mixture to a high-speed blender along with the maple syrup. Remove the center cap, cover with a kitchen towel to allow steam to escape, and blend until smooth. Blend on low and increase the speed until the mixture is creamy and smooth, about 2 minutes. Taste and adjust seasonings, if desired. Store in a sealed container in the refrigerator for up to 4 days or in the freezer for 4 months.

Yield: 4 cups (1,025 g)

Tip

If you prefer a traditional marinara, just leave out the beets and maple syrup. Create a spicy arrabbiata sauce by adding more crushed red pepper flakes until desired spice level is reached.

Create Your Epic

- Pizza Burrito Supreme (page 110)
- Stuffed-Crust Meatball Parm Pizza (page 112)
- Upside-Down Deep-Dish Pizza (page 114)
- Unicorn French Bread Pizza (page 118)

HOLLANDAISE FOR DAYS

I was staying at a cabin in the Catskills with my husband, David, early on in our relationship. David was not vegan at the time, and I was using every opportunity I could to wow him with food. I paired this sauce with the Eggsellent Eggs on page 32 on top of a toasted English muffin with some sautéed spinach, and it was a win! Need proof? He put a ring on it. May this sauce bring you as much joy as it has brought me … or at least be a nice addition to your breakfast now and then.

- 1 cup (225 g) vegan mayonnaise
- 3 tablespoons (42 g) vegan butter, melted
- 1 teaspoon lemon juice
- 1 teaspoon hot sauce
- ½ teaspoon ground turmeric
- ¼ teaspoon black pepper

In a bowl, whisk together the mayonnaise, butter, lemon juice, hot sauce, turmeric, and pepper until well combined. Store in a sealed container in the refrigerator for up to 1 week.

Yield: 1 cup (260 g)

Tip

The best part about this sauce—aside from it not using the butter and egg yolks of a traditional hollandaise—is how easy it is to make! There's no cooking involved, no chance for it separating, and it holds beautifully. Total win!

Create Your Epic

- Triple-Decker Brekky Sammy (page 88)

DREAMY CREAMY CREAM CHEESE

This cream cheese is the perfect base for the Crab Rangoon on page 30 or for your morning bagel. The addition of sauerkraut gives it that subtle push of sharp tanginess I'm always after! And it really makes the Loxed and Loaded Bagel Bites on page 83 come to life with the addition of scallions for a scallion cream cheese. No matter what way you choose to use it, the decadence of the cashews is certain to satisfy that cream-cheese craving.

- ▶ 1 cup (137 g) raw cashews, soaked in water overnight or boiled for 10 minutes and drained
- ▶ ½ cup (120 ml) unsweetened soy or almond milk
- ▶ Juice of 1 lemon
- ▶ 1 tablespoon (9 g) sauerkraut
- ▶ 1 tablespoon (16 g) white miso
- ▶ 1 tablespoon (7 g) onion powder
- ▶ ½ teaspoon sea salt
- ▶ ⅓ cup (33 g) chopped scallions (optional)

Add the cashews, milk, lemon juice, sauerkraut, miso, onion powder, and salt to a high-speed blender. Start blending on low speed and gradually increase the speed as more of the ingredients break down. This will take some time to get a nice smooth texture, but I promise you, it's worth it!

Periodically stop and scrape down the sides of the blender to make sure all of the ingredients are being incorporated. Be patient, and blend until smooth and creamy—it will take several minutes and some stopping and going.

Transfer the mixture to a bowl and stir in the scallions, if using, until well incorporated. Store in a sealed container in the refrigerator for up to 5 days.

Yield: 1½ cups (358 g)

Tip

The thickness and tanginess of the cream cheese increases slightly when refrigerated overnight or over a couple days, but it is delicious when eaten straight away too!

Create **Your Epic**

- ▶ Crab Rangoon (page 30)
- ▶ Loxed and Loaded Bagel Bites (page 83)

BLUE CHEESE DRESSING

In my last book, *The Simply Vegan Cookbook*, I went about the task of re-creating my all-time favorite, nostalgia-laden dressing: RANCH. For this book, I wanted to offer up its slightly more robust and tangier cousin, Blue Cheese. This dressing complements so many items, and it's nice to have an easy, go-to recipe for it on hand.

- ½ cup (115 g) vegan mayonnaise
- 3 tablespoons (45 g) tahini
- 2 tablespoons (32 g) white miso
- 2 tablespoons (28 ml) water
- Juice of ½ lemon
- 1 tablespoon plus 1 teaspoon (20 g) Dijon mustard
- 1 tablespoon (15 ml) apple cider vinegar
- 1 teaspoon garlic powder
- ½ teaspoon dried parsley
- ¼ teaspoon black pepper

Add the mayonnaise, tahini, miso, water, lemon juice, mustard, vinegar, and garlic powder to a high-speed blender. Blend until smooth. Add the parsley and black pepper, and pulse a few times until just combined and specks of the parsley and pepper are still visible. Store in a sealed container in the refrigerator for up to 2 weeks.

Yield: 1 cup (260 g)

Tip

If desired, add ¼ cup (56 g) crumbled extra-firm tofu for texture.

Create **Your** Epic

- Everything Buffalo Cauliflower Bites (page 84)
- Bacon Macaroni and Cheese BBQ Blue Burger (page 90)
- Almost Famous Buffalo Chicken Lasagna (page 126)

COCONUT-CHEDDAR FONDUE

When I was filming season 2 of *The Vegan Roadie*, I ate at a great place in Denver called City O' City. It had this incredible savory waffle with a coconut-cheddar fondue, and I was hell-bent on re-creating it. I share this recipe in the cooking classes I teach, and the reaction is always positive. I hope you feel the same way!

- ▸ 1 can (13.5 ounces/983 ml) full-fat unsweetened coconut milk
- ▸ ¼ cup (20 g) nutritional yeast
- ▸ 1 tablespoon (8 g) cornstarch
- ▸ 1 tablespoon (16 g) white miso
- ▸ ½ teaspoon garlic powder
- ▸ ½ teaspoon ground turmeric
- ▸ ½ teaspoon sea salt
- ▸ ¼ teaspoon onion powder

Add the coconut milk, nutritional yeast, cornstarch, miso, garlic powder, turmeric, salt, and onion powder to a high-speed blender. Blend 1 to 2 minutes, or until smooth and creamy.

Transfer the mixture to a small saucepan and bring to a gentle bubble over medium heat. Reduce the heat to low and simmer for 5 minutes, or until slightly thicker, stirring sporadically. Serve hot. Best if used immediately but will keep in the refrigerator in a sealed container for 4 days; reheat in a small saucepan over low heat when ready to use.

Yield: 1½ cups (350 g)

Tip

Use this for a fondue night and have fun using your favorite breads, veggies, and other fondue staples for dipping!

Create **Your** Epic

- ▸ Savory Cheddar Fondue Waffle Bowl (page 139)

THE CHEESIEST CHEESE SAUCE

I once was a close contender for a spot on the Food Network's show *The Great Food Truck Race*. If chosen to compete, I knew I wouldn't be able to rely on things like nutritional yeast and miso, which can be challenging to find sometimes. I set forth to create a cheese sauce with ingredients I knew I could find anywhere in the country so I could effectively compete in any given situation, and that's when I got obsessive about creating this recipe. It's so versatile; I hope you love it as much as I do!

- 2½ cups (570 ml) water
- 2 cups (10 ounces/340 g) peeled and cubed kabocha or butternut squash
- 1 large russet potato, peeled and cubed
- ¼ cup (50 g) arborio rice
- 2 tablespoons (30 ml) olive oil
- ½ cup (80 g) chopped onion
- ½ cup (75 g) chopped red bell pepper
- 4 cloves garlic, roughly chopped
- ½ cup (71 g) sauerkraut
- ¼ cup (60 g) tahini
- 2 tablespoons (30 g) Dijon mustard
- 1 tablespoon (15 ml) white wine vinegar
- 2½ teaspoons sea salt
- ½ teaspoon black pepper
- ½ teaspoon paprika

In a large saucepan, combine the water, squash, potato, and rice. Cover and bring to a boil. Reduce to a simmer and cook for 10 minutes, or until the squash is fork-tender. Do not drain the water.

Heat the olive oil in a medium skillet over medium heat. Add the onion, bell pepper, and garlic. Sauté for 3 to 5 minutes, or until soft and fragrant.

In a high-speed blender, combine the sauerkraut, tahini, mustard, vinegar, salt, black pepper, and paprika. Transfer the contents of the saucepan (including the water) and the contents of the skillet to the blender. Remove the plug from the lid of the blender and place a dish towel over the hole to allow steam to escape. Blend on low and increase the speed until the mixture is creamy and smooth, about 2 minutes. Serve warm on recipes as needed or toss it with steamed broccoli or your favorite vegetables!

Store in a sealed container in the refrigerator for up to 5 days. Reheat in a saucepan over low heat when needed.

Yield: 6 cups (1,425 g)

Tip

I prefer kabocha squash, as it is slightly richer in flavor and color, but if you can find only butternut squash, that works just as well—and you can sometimes find it already peeled and cubed in the grocery store!

Create **Your** Epic

- Easy Creamy Shells and Cheese (page 16)
- Philly Cheesesteaks (page 20)
- Chili Cheese Crispy Drive-Thru Potato Wedges with Quinoa Bacon Bits (page 26)
- Breakfast Nachos (page 78)
- Cheesesteak Pizza (page 115)
- Cheesesteak Baked Potato Bowl (page 147)

SAUCY MOZZARELLA

While it's nice that we can purchase vegan mozzarella shreds and blocks at many supermarkets these days, it's equally as nice to have the option to make mozzarella at home when in a pinch! I love to combine this sauce with some store-bought vegan mozzarella shreds, the Pizza Dough on page 57, and the Beet Marinara on page 40 for an easy cheese pizza! But this sauce has many other uses, as you will see in later chapters.

- ▶ 1 cup (137 g) raw cashews, soaked in water overnight or boiled for 10 minutes and drained
- ▶ ¾ cup (175 ml) water
- ▶ Juice of ½ lemon
- ▶ ¼ cup (35 g) sauerkraut
- ▶ 1 teaspoon garlic powder
- ▶ 1 teaspoon onion powder
- ▶ 1 teaspoon sea salt

In a high-speed blender, combine the cashews, water, lemon juice, sauerkraut, garlic powder, onion powder, and salt. Blend until creamy and smooth, about 2 minutes. Use as directed in recipes. Store in a sealed container in the refrigerator for up to 5 days.

Yield: 1½ cups (390 g)

Tip

To make fresh mozzarella, prepare a quart container with cold water and 1 teaspoon sea salt. Add the finished cashew mixture to a saucepan along with 1 tablespoon (24 g) agar agar powder and 2 tablespoons (15 g) tapioca starch or tapioca flour. Cook over medium-high heat for 5 minutes, stirring continuously with a wooden spoon, until the mixture thickens and pulls away from the sides of the pan. Use a melon baller or ice cream scoop to scoop out balls and add them to the salted water; let sit overnight in the fridge to solidify. Fresh mozz will keep up to 5 days in the brine, and it goes great on salads and sandwiches!

Create **Your** Epic

- ▶ Disco Pretzel Bites (page 77)
- ▶ Pizzabon (page 108)
- ▶ Franks 'n Mac Pizza (page 109)
- ▶ Crab Rangoon Pizza (page 116)
- ▶ Unicorn French Bread Pizza (page 118)
- ▶ French Onion Pasta Bake with Pizza Croutons (page 124)

SWEET THAI CHILI SAUCE

I have never been a fan of store-bought sweet Thai chili sauce; it always has a plastic aftertaste to me. But because I like the flavors of the sauce, it was imperative for me to create my own. The first version I created a few years ago was for Sweet Thai Chili Cauliflower Bites (see Tip) that I used to make in classes I taught. This recipe has gone through many incarnations, and I'm totally stoked to deliver it for you to have at home.

- ▶ 1 cup (225 g) packed organic light brown sugar

- ▶ ½ cup (120 ml) water, divided

- ▶ ¼ cup (60 ml) rice vinegar

- ▶ 2 cloves garlic, minced

- ▶ ½ teaspoon crushed red pepper flakes

- ▶ 2 tablespoons (16 g) cornstarch

- ▶ 1 tablespoon (15 g) ketchup

In a small saucepan, combine the brown sugar, ¼ cup (60 ml) of the water, rice vinegar, garlic, and crushed red pepper. Bring to a boil, then reduce to a simmer for 5 minutes, or until the sugar has completely dissolved.

In a small bowl, whisk together the cornstarch and remaining ¼ cup (60 ml) water to create a slurry. Whisk the slurry into the saucepan until well combined. Simmer for 2 to 4 minutes, until thickened. Whisk in the ketchup and transfer to a serving dish or use as needed in a recipe. Store in a sealed container in the refrigerator for up to 5 days.

Yield: 1 cup (300 g)

Tip

To make awesome Sweet Thai Chili Cauliflower Bites, toss this sauce with the cauliflower bites as prepared in the Everything Buffalo Cauliflower Bites recipe on page 84 and sprinkle with black or white sesame seeds.

Create Your Epic

- ▶ Sweet Thai Peanut Cauliflower Tacos (page 96)

- ▶ Crab Rangoon Pizza (page 116)

- ▶ Pad Thai Cupcakes (page 182)

MELLOW MUSHROOM GRAVY

I feel it's a requirement as a vegan to have a basic go-to gravy recipe on hand. I love this one because it is so easy, savory, and delicious. It pairs well with anything that calls for gravy but especially well with the Disco Pretzel Bites on page 77!

- 2 tablespoons (30 ml) olive oil
- ½ cup (80 g) chopped onion
- 1 package (8 ounces/227 g) baby bella or white button mushrooms, stemmed and roughly chopped
- 2 cloves garlic, minced
- 2 tablespoons (16 g) all-purpose flour
- 2 cups (475 ml) vegetable broth
- 1 tablespoon (15 ml) soy sauce
- ½ teaspoon sea salt
- ½ teaspoon black pepper

Heat the oil in a large skillet over medium-high heat. Add the onion and mushrooms. Sauté for 3 to 5 minutes, or until the onion is softened and the mushrooms have reduced in size slightly. Add the garlic and sauté for 1 additional minute, until fragrant.

Reduce the heat to medium and sprinkle the flour over the mixture. Toss with a spatula to coat everything with the flour. Slowly add the vegetable broth to the skillet and stir well. Add the soy sauce, salt, and pepper. Stir frequently for 3 to 5 minutes, or until the mixture has thickened and is lightly bubbling.

Serve as is, or transfer to a high-speed blender and blend until creamy and smooth, if desired.

Yield: 3 cups (610 g blended/ 680 g unblended)

Tip

This is my go-to gravy for holidays and any dinner served with mashed potatoes. I prefer to blend it all up for a saucier gravy, but if you prefer a slightly chunky mushroom gravy, blend half of it, return the blended half to the skillet, and stir together with the chunky gravy.

Create Your Epic

- Disco Pretzel Bites (page 77)

RED, WHITE, AND BBQ SAUCE

One summer I designed a menu with a friend of mine at her restaurant, Urban Vegan Kitchen in NYC, for a pop-up dinner with a BBQ theme. We wanted to include as many styles of BBQ sauce as we could on the menu. I'm delighted to offer a couple of the variations to you, as these BBQ sauces came about from nights of testing them over and over, making the smallest adjustments with my dear friend Pamela Elizabeth. Both are super tasty, but the white BBQ sauce won over the crowd at the dinner; hopefully it does the same for your hungry family and friends.

For Red BBQ Sauce:

- ▼ 2 tablespoons (30 ml) olive oil
- ▼ 1 onion, chopped
- ▼ 3 cloves garlic, chopped
- ▼ ½ cup (120 ml) bourbon
- ▼ 1 cup (240 g) ketchup
- ▼ ⅔ cup (160 ml) water, divided
- ▼ ¼ cup (60 g) organic dark brown sugar
- ▼ 2 tablespoons (16 g) chili powder
- ▼ 1 tablespoon (7 g) smoked paprika
- ▼ 1 tablespoon (15 g) Dijon mustard
- ▼ 1 tablespoon (15 ml) red wine vinegar
- ▼ 1 tablespoon (15 ml) molasses

For White BBQ Sauce:

- ▼ 1 cup (225 g) vegan mayonnaise
- ▼ 2 tablespoons (30 g) prepared horseradish
- ▼ 2 tablespoons (28 ml) agave
- ▼ 1 tablespoon (15 ml) distilled white vinegar
- ▼ 1 teaspoon garlic powder
- ▼ 1 teaspoon onion powder
- ▼ ¼ teaspoon sea salt
- ▼ ¼ teaspoon black pepper

To make the red BBQ sauce:

Heat the olive oil in a large skillet over medium heat. Sauté the onion for 3 to 5 minutes, or until softened. Add the garlic and sauté 1 additional minute, until fragrant. Slowly add the bourbon and cook for 4 to 6 minutes, or until the bourbon has completely cooked off.

Add the ketchup, ⅓ cup (80 ml) of the water, brown sugar, chili powder, smoked paprika, mustard, vinegar, and molasses. Stir well. Bring to a simmer and cook for 20 minutes, stirring occasionally. Transfer to a high-speed blender (see Tip), add the remaining ⅓ cup (80 ml) water, and blend until smooth.

To make the white BBQ sauce:

In a high-speed blender, combine the mayonnaise, horseradish, agave, vinegar, garlic powder, onion powder, salt, and pepper. Blend until smooth.

Store both sauces in sealed containers in the refrigerator for up to 1 week.

Yield: 1¼ cups (440 g) red, 1¼ cups (287 g) white

Tip

Blenders and heat don't mix! Either let the mixture cool completely before transferring to the blender, or remove the plug from the top of the blender and cover with a towel. Start blending on low and increase the speed until the mixture is smooth and creamy.

Create Your Epic

- ▼ Bacon Macaroni and Cheese BBQ Blue Burger (page 90)
- ▼ Grilled Romaine Bowl with White BBQ Sauce (page 148)

Pictured:
The Cheesiest Cheese Sauce; Avocado Sour Cream; Hollandaise for Days; Red, White, and BBQ Sauce; and Beet Marinara.

FUSS-FREE TARTAR SAUCE

I've been dumbfounded over people's efforts to create a vegan version of tartar sauce. The original tartar sauce is a mayonnaise base with just a touch of chopped pickled cucumber, aka gherkins (i.e., pickles). Seems simple enough, and this tartar sauce is just that, only with a relish so you don't even have to chop!

- ½ cup (115 g) vegan mayonnaise
- 2 tablespoons (30 g) sweet pickle relish

In a small bowl, stir together the mayonnaise and relish until well combined.

Yield: ½ cup (135 g)

Tip

Tartar sauce will keep in a sealed container in the refrigerator for up to 2 weeks.

Create **Your Epic**

- Jumbo Phish 'n Chips Sushi Roll (page 82)
- Hushpuppy Phish Fillet Sandwich (page 100)
- Mac Daddy Crunch Burrito (page 103)

AVOCADO SOUR CREAM

Avocados and sour cream have been appearing together on food since Sonny met Cher, probably even before that. I decided to combine the two for an easy no-muss, no-fuss recipe that gives me flavors from the best of both worlds! Use this recipe on everything you would use sour cream on: nachos, baked potatoes, tacos, or even as a tasty veggie dip!

- 1 avocado, peeled and cubed
- ¼ cup (60 ml) full-fat unsweetened coconut milk (the solid part from the can)
- 1 tablespoon (15 ml) apple cider vinegar
- ½ teaspoon sea salt
- ¼ cup (60 ml) water (as needed)

In a high-speed blender, combine the avocado, coconut milk, vinegar, and salt. Blend until smooth and creamy, adding a little water, 1 tablespoon (15 ml) at a time, if needed to reach desired consistency. Store in a sealed container in the refrigerator for 2 days.

Yield: ½ cup (120 g)

Tip

If you don't have a can of coconut milk on hand, you can substitute 2 tablespoons (28 ml) unsweetened soy or almond milk, but you will not likely need the water.

Create **Your Epic**

- Breakfast Nachos (page 78)
- Noritos Los Tacos (page 98)

CRACKLE AND FUDGY CHOCOLATE SAUCE

Eat your heart out, Dairy Queen: We got the crackle shell in full vegan force here. I love this on the Matcha Mint Pops with Pistachio Crunch Shell on page 170 so much, but it is perfect for any frozen treat you want to get that fun hard crackle shell on. For an extra treat, sprinkle it with Maldon or coarse sea salt (apply it quickly before it seizes up). And if you go with the fudgy option, it's like adding a layer of decadent chocolate to any cold treat!

- ▼ 1 cup (175 g) semi-sweet vegan chocolate chips
- ▼ ¼ cup (59 ml) unrefined coconut oil (for the crackle shell) or ¼ cup (59 ml) olive oil (for the fudgy sauce)
- ▼ ½ teaspoon sea salt

Melt the chocolate in a double boiler (see Tip). Add the oil and salt, gently whisking until fully melted and well combined. Remove from the heat.

Drizzle over frozen items, as desired. The crackle shell will seize up on contact. The fudgy sauce will get thicker and fudgier. Store sauces in sealed containers in the refrigerator for up to 2 weeks. Reheat either variation on the stovetop over low heat or in a microwave for 30-second intervals until melted and ready for use again.

Yield: 1 ¼ cups (400 g)

Tip

If you don't have a double boiler, you can easily create one with a medium saucepan and a stainless-steel or heat-resistant glass bowl that fits neatly into the saucepan. Fill the pan ¼ full with water and bring to a boil. Reduce to a simmer and fit the bowl into the pan; the bowl should not touch the water. Add the ingredients to the bowl and gently whisk until melted and smooth. The bowl will be hot, so use pot holders when handling.

Create **Your** Epic

- ▼ Matcha Mint Pops with Pistachio Crunch Shell (page 170)
- ▼ Churro Cup Sundaes (page 172)
- ▼ S'mores Cookie Cups (page 174)
- ▼ Power Tower Brownie Sundae (page 178)

SILKY SUNFLOWER CARAMEL SAUCE

Caramel can be a fussy little treat to make; between the sugar and the heat, it's easy to burn. Adding sunflower seed butter to the mix has made it a little less temperamental—not completely foolproof, but easier to manage than the traditional version with cream.

- ½ cup (100 g) organic cane sugar

- ½ cup (120 ml) unsweetened soy or almond milk

- ½ cup (130 g) sunflower seed butter, or nut butter of choice

- ¼ teaspoon sea salt

Combine the sugar and milk in a small saucepan over medium heat. Stir frequently for 2 minutes, or until the sugar has dissolved. Add the sunflower seed butter and salt, and stir until blended.

Reduce the heat to a simmer and stir frequently for 4 to 8 minutes, or until the sauce is thickened and sticks to the back of a spoon. Remove from the heat. Cooled caramel will keep in a sealed container in the refrigerator for up to 1 week.

Yield: 1 cup (295 g)

Tip

Be sure to remove the caramel from the heat right when it reaches the desired consistency! To reheat, bring it to a simmer in a small saucepan and remove from the heat as soon as it's fluid again and easily sticks to the back of a spoon but also slowly drips off the spoon.

Create Your Epic

- Ultimate Caramel Cookie Brownie Shake (page 152)

- Caramel-Stuffed Cookies 'n Cream Cupcakes (page 167)

- Churro Cup Sundaes (page 172)

- Sneaky Pickle Pineapple Ice Cream (page 175)

- Power Tower Brownie Sundae (page 178)

EASY WHIP 2 WAYS

I should call this "Granny's Vegan Whip" because the coconut version has been around since vegans were meeting in secret groups and making their own soymilk. The aquafaba, however, is fairly new, but it has turned into a bit of a craze. When something ain't broke, why fix it? The truth is, nothing gets fluffy like that gosh-darn aquafaba (the viscous liquid from a can of chickpeas). And nothing beats the creamy decadent indulgence of that coconut whip. So here they are, in one spot for you to choose from as you work your way through the milkshakes and desserts in this book. Be sure to reserve the chickpeas for the Keepin' It Clean Bowl on page 142.

For Aquafaba Whip:

▶ 2 cans (15 ounce/426 g) chickpeas

▶ ¼ cup (50 g) organic cane sugar

▶ 1 teaspoon vanilla extract

▶ ¼ teaspoon cream of tartar

For Coconut Whip:

▶ 2 cans (13.5 ounce/983 ml) full-fat unsweetened coconut milk, chilled overnight

▶ ¼ cup (30 g) organic confectioners' sugar

▶ 1 teaspoon vanilla extract

To make the aquafaba whip: Drain the aquafaba from the cans of chickpeas into the bowl of a stand mixer fitted with the whip attachment. (Reserve the chickpeas for another use.) Add the sugar, vanilla, and cream of tartar. Whip on medium speed for 5 minutes. Turn up the speed to high and whip for an additional 10 minutes, or until it gets even bigger and has fluffy peaks; it will triple in size.

The aquafaba whip will hold for about 1 hour. If you need it after that, rewhip it for 5 minutes, or until peaks form again. Store in a sealed container in the refrigerator for 3 days, and rewhip as needed.

To make the coconut whip: Put the mixing bowl of a stand mixer in the freezer for 20 minutes.

Carefully remove the lids of the coconut milk cans, without shaking them. Scoop out the solid part of the coconut milk and transfer it to the mixing bowl. (Reserve the liquid for smoothies.) Add the sugar and vanilla. Mix with the whip attachment for 2 to 4 minutes, starting at medium speed and increasing to high, until smooth and fluffy. Chill for 30 minutes before use. Store in a sealed container in the refrigerator for up to 1 week.

Yield: 8 cups (300 g) aquafaba whip and 1½ cups (56 g) coconut whip

Tip

Use a hand mixer for the coconut milk if need be, but a stand mixer is the best tool for either of these delicious treats to get a decadent fluffy whip!

Create **Your** Epic

▶ Several of the recipes in Chapter 9 (page 150)

▶ Churro Cup Sundaes (page 172)

▶ Power Tower Brownie Sundae (page 178)

BRAZEN BREADS:
All the Dough You Knead!

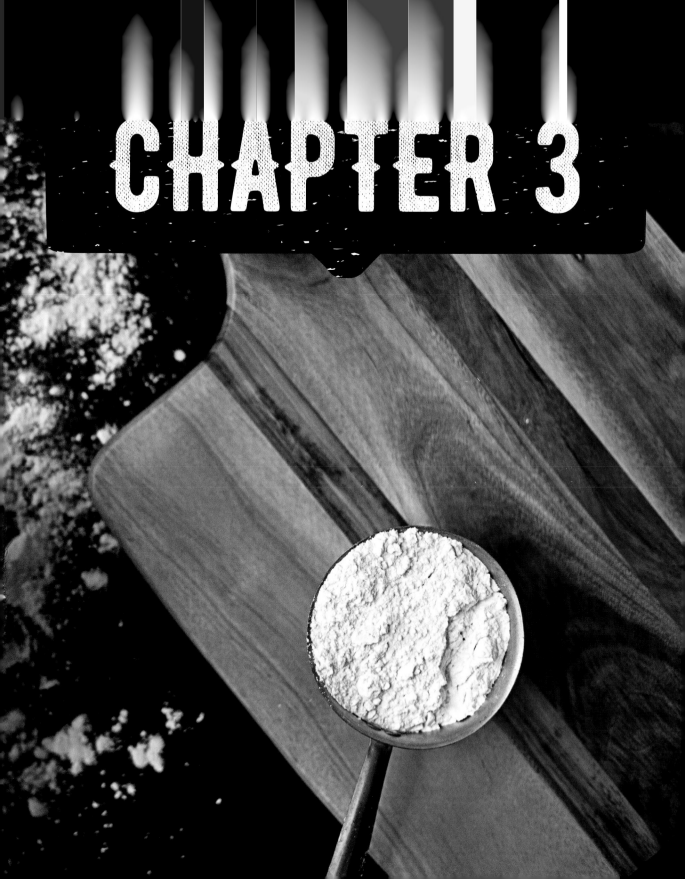

CHAPTER 3

CRAY CRAY BREAD

A very busy single mom raised me; she often had the Crock-Pot going, and we never lacked for a home-cooked meal. But occasionally, between running my sister and me around to practice and sports, I would get lucky with a stop at the Little Caesars drive-thru—yes, they had a drive-thru! And while I was excited about the pizza, it was the breadsticks that always had my mouth salivating that extra bit. This is an ode to those breadsticks. I like them with the Beet Marinara on page 40, but you can use your favorite dipping sauce.

- ▼ 1 cup (235 ml) warm water

- ▼ 2¼ teaspoons (5 g) active dry yeast (¼-ounce/7 g packet)

- ▼ 2 teaspoons (10 g) organic cane sugar

- ▼ 2½ cups (282 g) all-purpose flour

- ▼ 1 teaspoon sea salt

- ▼ Canola oil or cooking spray

- ▼ Stone-ground cornmeal or polenta (optional)

- ▼ 2 tablespoons (28 g) vegan butter, melted

- ▼ 1 teaspoon garlic powder

- ▼ 2 tablespoons (20 g) Hemp Parmesan (page 14), or store-bought vegan parmesan

In a mixing bowl, or in the bowl of a stand mixer fitted with the dough hook, whisk together the water, yeast, and sugar. Set aside for 10 minutes, until foamy.

Add the flour and salt. Using your hands or the dough hook, mix until all of the ingredients are well combined. Continue to knead with the dough hook on medium speed for 3 minutes or turn out onto a floured surface and knead with your hands for 5 minutes, until the dough is smooth and elastic.

Line a 9 x 12-inch (23 x 30-cm) baking sheet with parchment paper. Lightly coat with canola oil or cooking spray. Sprinkle with the cornmeal or polenta, if using. On the prepared baking sheet, gently roll or stretch the dough to the edges to create a 9 x 12-inch (23 x 30-cm) rectangle. (If you don't have a baking sheet this small, simply stretch the dough out to 9 x 12 inches [23 x 30 cm] on a larger baking sheet.)

Using a pizza cutter or sharp knife, slice the dough down the middle, then across 5 times to form 12 sticks. Cover with a clean kitchen towel and let rest for 10 minutes.

Meanwhile, preheat the oven to 450°F (230°C, or gas mark 8).

In a small bowl, combine the butter and garlic powder.

Bake the sticks for 6 to 8 minutes, or until golden brown. Remove from the oven and immediately brush the sticks with the butter mixture, then sprinkle with the parmesan. Serve warm.

Yield: 12 sticks

Tip

Using the cornmeal gets you closer to replicating the fast-food version of these well-known sticks.

PIZZA DOUGH

I LOVE PIZZA. It's my favorite food, hands down. I actually prefer a very basic pizza with crust, sauce, and cheese. And I love using the Beet Marinara on page 40 with the Saucy Mozzarella on page 45 for a delicious and easy combo that I'm very nostalgic for when it comes to pizza. Topped with some Hemp Parmesan (page 14), you can't go wrong! But you are the chef; use this crust and dive into the "Pizza! Pizza!" chapter (page 104), or create your own with your favorite toppings.

- 1½ cups (355 ml) warm water

- 2¼ teaspoons (5 g) active dry yeast (¼-ounce/7 g packet)

- 1 teaspoon organic cane sugar

- 4½ cups (564 g) all-purpose flour

- 1 teaspoon sea salt

- 2 tablespoons (40 g) maple syrup

- 1 tablespoon (15 ml) olive oil

In a medium bowl, whisk together the water, yeast, and sugar. Set aside for 10 minutes, until foamy.

In a large bowl, or in the bowl of a stand mixer fitted with the dough hook, combine the flour, salt, maple syrup, and olive oil. Add the yeast mixture. Mix until well combined using a wooden spoon or the dough hook on low speed. If the dough is too sticky, add more flour, 1 tablespoon (15 ml) at a time as needed, and knead the dough for about 3 minutes, until a stiff ball of dough has formed.

Coat the dough on all sides with the olive oil and place in a clean bowl. Cover with a clean kitchen towel and let rest in a warm place for 1 hour, or until doubled in size.

Punch down the dough and turn it out onto a floured surface. Cut the dough in half and stretch or roll out the dough according to a recipe, as needed. Store unused dough, wrapped in plastic wrap or large resealable plastic bags with the air pressed out, in the refrigerator for up to 4 days. But for best results, use the dough when it is fresh.

Yield: Two 12-inch (30-cm) pizza crusts

Tip

Be mindful that this recipe makes enough dough for TWO PIZZAS. For recipes that call for Pizza Dough, split this dough in half and use one half for one pizza. But let's be real: Who is going to wait to use that second half?! Use it to create a second pizza from this book, or customize a pizza with your favorite toppings, then invite your neighbors over for a pizza party! Provided you like your neighbors.

Create **Your** Epic

- Festive Cheesy Spinach Bread (page 53)

- Franks 'n Mac Pizza (page 109)

- Pizza Burrito Supreme (page 110)

- Stuffed-Crust Meatball Parm Pizza (page 112)

- Upside-Down Deep-Dish Pizza (page 114)

- Crab Rangoon Pizza (page 116)

FESTIVE CHEESY SPINACH BREAD

I served this bread at a holiday party to a room full of nonvegans, and it was a hit! It's a fun recipe to bring to the table, and once people are done "oohing" and "ahhing" over how fun it looks, they will be delighted to find out it's just as fun to eat. And don't freak out—it's easier than it looks! In the words of Carla, one of the amazing recipe testers for this book, "This is a total showstopper. One of those recipes that looked like it took a ton of time to make, but is actually super easy." So listen to Carla: It's easy! I must mention to be mindful to really squeeze that spinach dry to avoid extra moisture.

- ½ cup (68 g) raw cashews, soaked in water overnight or boiled for 10 minutes and drained
- ¼ cup plus 2 tablespoons (88 ml) water
- 2 tablespoons (10 g) nutritional yeast
- 2 teaspoons (10 ml) lemon juice
- 1 clove garlic
- ½ teaspoon onion powder
- ½ teaspoon sea salt
- ½ cup (58 g) vegan cheddar shreds
- ¼ cup (20 g) packed frozen chopped spinach, thawed and squeezed dry (see Tip on page 122)
- 1 batch Pizza Dough (page 57), divided, enough for 1 pizza (see Tip on page 57)

- 2 tablespoons (42 g) vegan butter, melted
- ½ teaspoon garlic powder
- ½ teaspoon Italian seasoning
- Maldon or coarse sea salt (optional)
- Beet Marinara (page 40), for dipping
- Blue Cheese Dressing (page 42), for dipping

Preheat the oven to 400°F (200°C, or gas mark 6). Line a large baking sheet (13 x 18 inches [33 x 46 cm] or larger) with parchment paper.

In a high-speed blender, combine the cashews, water, nutritional yeast, lemon juice, garlic, onion powder, and salt. Blend until creamy and smooth, 1 to 2 minutes. Transfer to a bowl, and stir in the cheese and spinach. Set aside.

Take the parchment from the baking sheet and lay it on a flat surface. Roll out the pizza dough to a 10 x 12-inch (26 x 30-cm) rectangle on the parchment paper. With a pizza cutter or sharp knife, cut the dough into the shape of a tree with the tip at the top; keep the excess dough where it lays—don't gather it or remove it from the parchment. Carefully transfer the parchment paper with the dough on it back to the baking sheet.

Spread the spinach mixture over the tree part of the dough, leaving a ½-inch (1-cm) border all around the tree dough. Flip the 2 pieces of dough that were cut off from the sides, so that the bottom points are now up top, and lay the pieces over the filling

to match the shape of the tree and cover the filling. Pinch the 2 pieces of the top layer of dough together in the middle and pinch all sides of the dough together to close in the filling.

Cut 7 lines, through to the bottom, from either side of the dough toward the middle of the tree, being careful to leave the dough connected in the middle; there will be 8 "tree branches" on each side. Twist each branch toward the bottom one time.

Bake for 20 to 22 minutes, or until crispy and golden brown. While it's baking, mix together the butter, garlic powder, and Italian seasoning. When the bread is done, remove from the oven and immediately brush with the butter mixture. Sprinkle with the coarse salt, if desired.

Serve warm with the Beet Marinara and Blue Cheese Dressing for dipping.

Yield: 16 pieces

Tip

Not a holiday, but you still want the festive bread? No prob! Just roll out the rectangle, spread the filling on half (widthwise), then fold the dough in half over the filling and pinch the edges closed. Cut lines to create the "tree branches" without the tree shape for the perfect spinach-stuffed breadsticks!

Short on time and need to skip the from-scratch dough? I got you. Use 11 to 13 ounces (312 to 368 g) of any store-bought dough—just be sure to check the ingredients label first.

PRETZEL DOUGH

When I was in high school, we had à la carte stations in addition to the standard lunch line. It wasn't as fancy as it sounds—don't get too excited—but we did have these huge pretzel buns that everyone loved. I also had a fondness for Auntie Anne's pretzel bites. Come to think of it, I'm a fan of the classic NYC street pretzel, too! Well, with this recipe you can have all three! What sets apart a pretzel dough from any other yeast dough is the brief stop in a hot baking soda bath. Don't be intimidated, though; think of it as a spa date for the pretzels. I know once you master these, your pretzel game will be strong.

- 2 cups (475 ml) warm water
- 2¼ teaspoons (5 g) active dry yeast (¼-ounce/7 g packet)
- 1 teaspoon organic cane sugar
- 5 cups (625 g) all-purpose flour
- 1 cup (80 g) nutritional yeast
- 1 teaspoon sea salt
- Canola oil
- 8 cups (1.9 l) water
- ¼ cup (60 g) baking soda
- ½ cup (112 g) vegan butter, melted
- Maldon or coarse sea salt

In a medium bowl, whisk together the water, yeast, and sugar. Set aside for 10 minutes, until foamy.

In a large bowl, or in the bowl of a stand mixer fitted with the dough hook, combine the flour, nutritional yeast, and sea salt. Add the yeast-water mixture and mix everything together with your hands or the dough hook, adding more water, 1 tablespoon (15 ml) at a time if necessary, until the dough just comes together to form a ball.

Knead the dough in the mixer for 3 minutes or with your hands on a floured surface for 5 minutes, or until a firm, elastic ball forms. Coat the ball on all sides with canola oil and place in a large clean bowl. Cover with a clean kitchen towel and let rest in a warm place for 1 hour, or until doubled in size.

Preheat the oven to 425°F (220°C, or gas mark 7). Line a baking sheet with parchment paper.

Bring the water to boil in a stockpot. Add the baking soda, 1 tablespoon (15 g) at a time, as the water will foam when it's added.

To make the pretzel bowls:

Punch down the dough, turn it out onto a floured surface, and knead for 2 minutes until a firm ball forms; cut into 4 equal-size pieces. Form each piece into a ball that is 2 inches (5 cm) thick and 4 inches (10 cm) in diameter.

Transfer 1 dough ball to the boiling water and boil for 1 minute. Remove with a slotted spoon and transfer to the prepared baking sheet. Repeat with the remaining balls of dough.

Gently brush each bowl with the butter and sprinkle with the coarse salt. Bake for 14 to 16 minutes, or until golden brown.

When cool enough to handle, create a bowl by cutting out the center with a knife; cut deep enough to create a bowl, but be careful to leave the edge thick enough to hold liquid. Once you have removed the top you can continue to scrape the inside out with a spoon to create a deeper bowl, taking care not to puncture the edge so the bowl can hold soup. You can start munching on those bits of pretzel from the top of the bowls if you can't resist, or use them to dip in the soup or even as the croutons in the Pizza Croutons (page 124).

To make the pretzel bites:

Punch down the dough, turn it out onto a floured surface, and knead for 2 minutes until a firm ball forms; cut into 4 equal-size pieces, then cut each piece in half. Roll each piece between your hands and the floured surface to create a 12-inch (30-cm) rope. Cut each rope into 1-inch (2.5-cm) nuggets; you will have 12 nuggets from each rope.

Transfer the nuggets to the boiling water, 6 at a time, and boil for 1 minute. Remove with a slotted spoon and transfer to the prepared baking sheet. Repeat with the remaining nuggets.

Gently brush each bite with the butter and sprinkle with the coarse salt. Bake for 12 to 14 minutes, or until golden brown.

To make the soft pretzels:

Punch down the dough, turn it out onto a floured surface, and knead for 2 minutes until a firm ball forms; cut into 4 equal-size pieces. Roll each piece between your hands and the floured surface to create a 21-inch (53-cm) rope.

Form a U-shape with the rope. Holding the ends of the rope, cross them over each other, then twist them once around. Press the tips down onto the bottom of the U in order to form the shape of a pretzel. (For a little assistance, search YouTube, and you will soon be a graduate of Soft Pretzel University!)

Carefully transfer the pretzel to the boiling water and boil for 1 minute. Remove with a slotted spoon and transfer to the prepared baking sheet. Repeat with the remaining pretzels.

Carefully brush each pretzel with the butter and sprinkle with the coarse salt. Bake for 13 to 15 minutes, or until golden brown.

Yield: 4 bowls, 96 bites, or 4 soft pretzels

Tip

Have fun with toppings for these! Some of my favorites are everything-spice mix (page 84), cinnamon-sugar (page 172), or even simple nutritional yeast instead of just salt. Pretzels are also great for dipping in sauces like Blue Cheese Dressing (page 42), Coconut-Cheddar Fondue (page 43), or The Cheesiest Cheese Sauce (page 44).

Create Your Epic

▶ Mac and Cheese Pretzel Bites (page 76)

▶ Disco Pretzel Bites (page 77)

▶ Loaded Baked Potato Soup with Pretzel Bowls (page 140)

CORNBREAD CROUTONS

I was working on a pop-up dinner and needed something for an over-the-top grilled salad featuring corn. I wanted cornbread, but I didn't want it to be a basic slab of cornbread, so I created a super simple cornbread crouton. This tasty morsel delivers just the right bit of savory crunch to any salad (or soup!). And if you feel more like being "basic," there's no judgment here! See the Tip for how to make a basic cornbread fit for any occasion.

- ▼ 1½ cups (210 g) stone-ground yellow cornmeal

- ▼ 1 cup (125 g) all-purpose flour

- ▼ 6 tablespoons (78 g) organic cane sugar

- ▼ 1 teaspoon baking soda

- ▼ 1½ teaspoons sea salt, divided

- ▼ 2 cups (475 ml) unsweetened soy or almond milk

- ▼ 1 tablespoon (15 ml) apple cider vinegar

- ▼ ⅓ cup (79 ml) canola oil

- ▼ ¼ cup (55 g) vegan butter, melted

- ▼ ¼ teaspoon black pepper

Preheat the oven to 400°F (200°C, or gas mark 6). Line a shallow 16 x 12-inch (40 x 30-cm) baking sheet with parchment paper.

In a large bowl, whisk together the cornmeal, flour, sugar, baking soda, and 1 teaspoon of the salt. Add the milk, vinegar, and canola oil. Whisk until everything is just incorporated; do not overmix. Pour the mixture onto the prepared baking sheet. Bake for 14 to16 minutes, or until the edges are just starting to brown.

While the cornbread bakes, combine the butter, pepper, and remaining ½ teaspoon salt in a bowl and mix well.

Remove the cornbread from the oven and cut into 1-inch (2.5-cm) cubes, or desired size. Transfer the cubes to a bowl, drizzle with the butter mixture, and toss until well coated. Transfer back to the parchment-lined baking sheet, and bake for 4 to 6 minutes, or until browned and crispy.

Yield: about 6 cups (1,207 g) croutons

Tip

To make classic cornbread, follow the instructions as written, but bake in a lightly greased 8-inch (20-cm) square baking pan for 20 to 22 minutes, or until the edges start to brown and the top cracks. Omit the final butter-salt-pepper step and cut into 16 pieces.

Create Your Epic

- ▼ Bless-Your-Heart Bowl (page 146)

- ▼ Grilled Romaine Bowl with White BBQ Sauce (page 148)

MONTE CRISTO ROLLS

The Monte Cristo is essentially a grilled turkey, ham, and cheese sandwich, typically dipped in egg before it hits the pan. This mashup drops the egg but adds cinnamon rolls; it will have friends and family going bananas if you pull these out for brunch. The savory and sweet combination, with the addition of the raspberry preserves, is a combination that will have everyone wanting seconds!

- ▼ Canola oil or cooking spray

- ▼ 1 batch Cinnadiction Rolls dough, proofed and ready to be turned out (page 66)

- ▼ ¾ cup (240 g) plus 2 tablespoons (40 g) raspberry preserves, divided

- ▼ 6 slices vegan American cheese

- ▼ 12 slices vegan deli ham

- ▼ 6 slices vegan provolone cheese

- ▼ 12 slices vegan deli turkey

- ▼ 1 tablespoon (15 ml) water

- ▼ Organic confectioners' sugar

Lightly coat a 9 x 13-inch (23 x 33-cm) baking dish with canola oil or cooking spray.

Roll out the dough on a lightly floured surface into a 16 x 12-inch (40 x 30-cm) rectangle, about ¼ inch (6 mm) thick, with the long edge toward you.

Spread ¾ cup (240 g) of the raspberry preserves over the dough. Place the American cheese slices along the bottom to create a row. Create a row above the cheese by placing 6 slices of the ham on the dough, then top each slice of ham with a second slice of ham. Repeat with the provolone and turkey to create two more rows that will cover all the dough.

Roll up the dough from the bottom to the top as tightly and evenly as possible; set it on its seam. Cut the dough into 12 equal pieces, about 1½ inches (3.5 cm) thick.

Place the rolls, cut-sides up, into the prepared pan. There should be 4 rows with 3 rolls in each, with some space between each roll. Cover with a clean kitchen towel and let rest in a warm place for about 20 minutes, or until they have risen and expanded. While they are rising, preheat the oven to 350°F (175°C, or gas mark 4).

Bake for 35 to 40 minutes, or until the tops are lightly browned. Let cool in the dish for 15 minutes.

In a small bowl, whisk together the remaining 2 tablespoons (40 g) raspberry preserves and water until well combined; drizzle sparingly over the top of the rolls. Sift confectioners' sugar over the top before serving warm.

Yield: 12 rolls

Tip

Don't stress out trying to find the exact vegan cheese slices called for here; they aren't widely available—yet. But many are, so find two cheeses you like and use those!

Cinnadiction Rolls, page 66

Monte Cristo Rolls, page 63

CINNADICTION ROLLS

Cinnamon rolls are everyone's decadent sinful delight. That cinnamon roll kiosk at the mall everyone loved in the '90s, Cinnabon, is the inspiration for this roll. While they can be intimidating to tackle, nothing feels as satisfying as serving up warm homemade cinnamon rolls to your brunch guests. Just take your time and go step by step: While the dough is resting, make the filling; while the baked rolls are cooling, make the icing. Or assemble them the night before (see Tip).

For Dough:

- 1 cup (235 ml) plus ¼ cup (60 ml) warm water, divided
- 2¼ teaspoons (5 g) active dry yeast (¼-ounce/7 g packet)
- 1 teaspoon (4 g) plus ½ cup (100 g) organic cane sugar, divided
- 2 tablespoons (14 g) flax meal
- 4 cups (500 g) all-purpose flour
- ⅓ cup (75 g) vegan butter, melted
- 1 teaspoon sea salt
- Canola oil or cooking spray

For Filling:

- 1 cup (225 g) packed organic dark brown sugar
- ½ cup (112 g) vegan butter, melted
- 3 tablespoons (21 g) ground cinnamon

For Icing:

- 1½ cups (150 g) organic confectioners' sugar
- 6 tablespoons (84 g) vegan butter, room temperature
- ¼ cup (60 g) vegan cream cheese, room temperature
- ½ teaspoon vanilla extract
- 2 pinches sea salt

To make the dough: In a medium bowl, whisk together 1 cup (235 ml) of the water, yeast, and 1 teaspoon of the cane sugar. Set aside for 10 minutes, until foamy.

In a small bowl, combine the flax meal and remaining ¼ cup (60 ml) water. Set aside for 5 minutes, until thickened.

In a large bowl, or in the bowl of a stand mixer fitted with the dough hook, combine the remaining ½ cup (100 g) sugar, flour, butter, and salt. Add the yeast mixture and the flax mixture. Mix until everything just comes together. Knead on a floured surface or with the dough hook for 2 to 4 minutes, until a stiff, elastic dough forms. Coat the dough on all sides with canola oil and place in a clean bowl. Cover with a clean kitchen towel and let rest in a warm place for 1 hour, or until doubled in size.

Lightly coat a 9 x 13-inch (23 x 33-cm) baking dish with canola oil or cooking spray.

Punch down the dough and turn it out onto a lightly floured surface. Roll it into a 16 x 12-inch (40 x 30-cm) rectangle, about ¼ inch (6 mm) thick, with the long edge toward you.

To make the filling: In a small bowl, mix together the brown sugar, butter, and cinnamon. Spread the filling evenly over the surface of the dough. Roll up the dough from the bottom to the top as tightly and evenly as possible; set it on its seam. Cut the dough into 12 equal pieces, about 1½ inches (3.5 cm) thick.

Place the rolls, cut-sides up, into the prepared baking dish. There should be 4 rows with 3 rolls in each, with some space between each roll. Cover with a clean kitchen towel and let rest in a warm place for about 20 minutes, or until they have risen and expanded. While they are rising, preheat the oven to 350°F (175°C, or gas mark 4).

Bake for 20 to 25 minutes, or until the tops are lightly browned. Let cool in the baking dish for 30 minutes.

To make the icing: In a medium bowl with a hand mixer, or the bowl of a stand mixer fitted with the paddle attachment, combine the confectioners' sugar, butter, cream cheese, vanilla, and salt. Mix until creamy and smooth, 1 to 2 minutes.

Spread the icing over the tops of the rolls; it will melt a little. Dig in right away, but they're better if you let the rolls sit for an additional 20 to 25 minutes for the icing to solidify.

Bacon variation: Use 1 cup (160 g) Quinoa Bacon Bits (page 14) and sprinkle ¾ cup (120 g) over the cinnamon-sugar spread before rolling up the dough. Sprinkle the remaining ¼ cup (40 g) over the rolls once they've been iced.

Yield: 12 rolls

Tip

Make-ahead hack: After the assembled, but unbaked, rolls have risen, cover the baking dish with plastic wrap and refrigerate overnight. The next day, remove the wrap, allow to come to room temperature, and bake according to recipe instructions.

Create Your Epic

▸ Monte Cristo Rolls (page 63)

▸ Bacon–Cinnamon Roll Burger with Peanut Butter (page 92)

▸ Pizzabon (page 108)

GARLICKY CHEDDAR BISCUITS WITH SAUSAGE GRAVY

Biscuits and gravy is one of my favorite vegan diner dishes, and aren't we blessed to have so many vegan diners popping up all over the United States? But I always felt the gravy was the star of this dish, no matter how good the biscuits were, so I wanted to offer up a biscuit that complemented the gravy just as much as the gravy complemented the biscuit—and this recipe delivers. What's even better is that you can serve these biscuits by themselves because they are jam-packed full of flavor!

For Biscuits:

- ¾ cup (175 ml) unsweetened soy or almond milk
- Juice of ½ lemon
- 2 cups (250 g) all-purpose flour
- 1 tablespoon (13 g) organic cane sugar
- 1 tablespoon (14 g) baking powder
- 2 teaspoons garlic powder
- ¼ teaspoon cayenne pepper
- ½ cup (112 g) vegan butter
- 1½ cups (173 g) vegan cheddar shreds

For Garlicky Topping:

- 3 tablespoons (42 g) vegan butter, melted
- 2 teaspoons dried parsley
- 1 teaspoon garlic powder

For Gravy:

- 2 tablespoons (30 ml) olive oil
- 2 vegan sausages, ground or diced small
- ½ large onion, chopped
- 2 cloves garlic, minced
- 2 tablespoons (16 g) all-purpose flour
- 1½ cups (355 ml) unsweetened soy or almond milk
- ¾ teaspoon sea salt
- ½ teaspoon black pepper
- ¼ teaspoon chili powder

For Garnish:

- Chopped chives or fresh parsley

To make the biscuits: Preheat the oven to 400°F (200°C, or gas mark 6). Line a baking sheet with parchment paper.

In a small bowl, combine the milk with the lemon juice. Let it sit for 5 minutes until it thickens.

In a medium bowl, whisk together the flour, sugar, baking powder, garlic powder, and cayenne pepper. Cut the butter into the flour mixture with a fork, pastry cutter, or your fingers until it develops a crumbly, sand-like consistency. Mix in the cheese, then add the milk mixture. Mix with a spatula until everything is well combined; the dough will seem slightly wet, but don't overmix.

Using a ¼ cup measuring cup, scoop out 12 portions onto the prepared baking sheet, setting them at least ½ inch (1 cm) apart. Bake for 14 to 16 minutes, or until the tops look dry and the bottoms are just slightly browned.

To make the garlicky topping: In a small bowl, combine the butter, parsley, and garlic powder. When the biscuits come out of the oven, immediately brush the tops with the butter mixture.

To make the gravy: While the biscuits bake, heat the oil in a large skillet over medium heat. Add the sausages and onion. Sauté for 3 to 4 minutes, or until the sausages are browned and the onions are softened. Add the garlic and sauté an additional 1 minute, until fragrant.

Sprinkle the flour over the sausage mixture in the skillet and toss with a spatula to coat everything with the flour. Slowly add the milk, stirring until incorporated. Bring just to a bubble and lower the heat to a simmer. Add the salt, pepper, and chili powder. Simmer 2 to 4 minutes, or until the gravy thickens more. Taste and add more seasoning, if desired.

Plate 2 biscuits and smother with ⅓ cup (80 ml) gravy. Garnish with chopped chives or fresh parsley, if desired.

Yield: 6 servings (12 biscuits, 2 cups [475 ml] gravy)

Tip

Don't have sausage? No problem! Omit the sausage and just call it "country gravy"; adjust seasoning, if desired.

Create bite-size portions of these biscuits by dropping 1 heaping tablespoon of the dough onto a prepared baking sheet about 1 inch (2.5 cm) apart and bake for 8 to 10 minutes. They are great for holiday gatherings.

Create **Your** Epic

▼ Lobster Roll 'n a Biscuit Sliders (page 92)

▼ Deep-Dish Brunch Pizza (page 106)

SWEET POTATO WAFFLES WITH CARDAMOM BUTTER

These are the waffles you serve at your brunch party to impress your pretentious foodie friends. You don't even need to give me credit; take it all for yourself, bask in the glory of your guests enjoying every bite, and soak up the compliments that come in. No need to tell them how easy it was to pull it all together, and you get bonus points for feigning that you slaved all morning in the kitchen. These pair nicely with the Blood Orange Mimosa Float on page 162, served up for brunch dessert. If you don't have a waffle maker, no sweat, this batter can be used to make fluffy pancakes instead!

For Butter:

▼ ½ cup (112 g) vegan butter, room temperature

▼ ½ teaspoon ground cardamom

For Waffles:

▼ 2 cups (250 g) all-purpose flour

▼ 2 tablespoons (28 g) baking powder

▼ 1 teaspoon sea salt

▼ 1½ cups (338 g) cooked and mashed sweet potato

▼ 1 cup (235 ml) unsweetened soy or almond milk

▼ ¾ cup (175 ml) orange juice

▼ 2 tablespoons (40 g) maple syrup

▼ 2 tablespoons (30 ml) vanilla extract

▼ 1 teaspoon ground nutmeg

To make the butter: In a small bowl, whisk together the butter and cardamom until well combined. Place in the refrigerator to harden a bit before serving.

To make the waffles: Preheat and coat the waffle iron according to the manufacturer's instructions.

In a large bowl, whisk together the flour, baking powder, and salt. Add the sweet potato, milk, orange juice, maple syrup, vanilla, and nutmeg. Whisk until well combined, but do not overmix.

Cook the waffles according to the waffle maker's instructions. Be sure to get a nice crisp outside on the waffle to give it some structure.

Yield: 4 to 6 waffles, depending on waffle maker

Tip

Make the butter a day ahead to have cold cardamom butter to serve with the hot waffles. A melon baller is the perfect tool to scoop out uniform balls of butter for each waffle. The waffles also freeze well. Wrap any leftover waffles tightly in plastic wrap and freeze for up to 2 weeks. Reheat by placing them on a baking sheet and baking at 350°F (175°C, or gas mark 4) for 8 to 10 minutes, or until heated through.

Create Your Epic

▼ Fried Chicken 'n Waffle Benedict Sandwich (page 99)

▼ Savory Cheddar Fondue Waffle Bowl (page 139)

CRISPY CREAM DONUTS

One would think that a donut company that was founded in 1937 would have had the wherewithal to create a vegan version of their popular donut by now, but no such luck. That's what I'm here for! These are ridiculously addicting with the traditional glaze, but get crafty and mix it up with the chocolate glaze and your favorite toppings.

For Donuts:

- ¼ cup (60 ml) plus 2 tablespoons (28 ml) water, divided
- 2¼ teaspoons (5 g) active dry yeast (¼-ounce/7 g packet)
- 1 teaspoon (4 g) plus ¼ cup (50 g) organic cane sugar, divided
- 1 tablespoon (7 g) flax meal
- ¼ cup (55 g) vegan butter, room temperature
- ¾ cup (175 ml) unsweetened soy or almond milk
- 1 teaspoon vanilla extract
- 3 cups (375 g) all-purpose flour
- Canola oil

For Traditional Glaze:

- 1½ cups (150 g) organic confectioners' sugar
- ½ cup (112 g) vegan butter, melted
- ¼ cup (80 g) maple syrup
- 2 teaspoons vanilla extract

For Chocolate Glaze:

- 1 cup (120 g) organic confectioners' sugar
- 2 tablespoons (10 g) unsweetened cocoa powder
- 1 tablespoon (15 ml) plus 2 teaspoons unsweetened soy or almond milk
- ½ to 1 cup sprinkles, shredded coconut, or chopped nuts

To make the donuts: In a small bowl, whisk together ¼ cup (235 ml) of the water, yeast, and 1 teaspoon of the cane sugar. Set aside for 10 minutes, until foamy.

In a separate small bowl, combine the flax meal and remaining 2 tablespoons (28 ml) of water. Set aside for 5 minutes, until thickened.

In a large bowl with a hand mixer, or in the bowl of a stand mixer fitted with the paddle attachment, cream together the butter with the remaining ¼ cup (50 g) cane sugar until well combined. Add the yeast mixture, flax mixture, milk, and vanilla. Mix until well combined. Add the flour and mix (using the dough hook or a wooden spoon) until just combined. If the dough is sticky, add 1 tablespoon (8 g) flour, as needed, until a smooth ball forms.

Knead for 2 to 4 minutes, either by hand or with the mixer on medium speed, until the dough is elastic and firm. Coat the ball on all sides with canola oil. Place the ball in a clean bowl and cover with a clean kitchen towel. Let rest in a warm place for 1 hour, or until doubled in size.

Punch down the dough and turn out onto a well-floured surface. Roll out to a 9 x 12-inch (23 x 30-cm) rectangle, ½ inch (1 cm) thick, but do not overwork the dough; it should remain light and fluffy. Use a donut cutter to cut out donut shapes (see Tip on page 72). Collect the leftover dough scraps into a ball, roll to ½ inch (1 cm) thick, and cut out more donuts. Continue until all the scraps have been used. Cover with

(continued)

a clean kitchen towel and let rest 30 minutes, or until doubled in size.

In a large skillet, pour ½ inch (1 cm) of canola oil. Heat the oil to 350°F (175°C) when tested with a candy thermometer or until bubbles form around the handle of a wooden spoon when inserted into the oil. Line a baking sheet or cooling rack with paper towels.

Carefully transfer the donuts to the oil, 2 or 3 at a time. Fry for 20 to 25 seconds, or until golden, on each side, using tongs to flip. Transfer to the prepared baking sheet or cooling rack. Allow the donuts to cool for 10 minutes.

To make the traditional glaze: In a medium bowl, whisk together the confectioners' sugar, butter, maple syrup, and vanilla until smooth and creamy.

Once the donuts have cooled enough to handle, place them 1 at a time in the glaze, flipping with tongs until the donut is fully coated, and set on a cooling rack. Let the glaze set for 15 minutes, or until it has dried. Be sure to set paper towels, a cutting board or waxed paper under the cooling rack to catch the glaze drippings!

To make the chocolate glaze: In a small bowl, whisk together the confectioners' sugar and cocoa powder. Add the milk, and whisk until smooth and creamy.

Pour sprinkles, coconut, or nuts into a bowl or shallow plate.

Dip the top of a donut into the glaze, thoroughly coating the top, then dip the glazed part into the sprinkles, coconut, or nuts, covering generously. Transfer to a cooling rack, and let sit for 15 minutes for the glaze to set.

Yield: 18 to 22 donuts

Tip

If you don't have a donut cutter, use the rim of a pint glass to cut out the donut and then the rim of a baby food jar (or something comparable in size) to cut the hole from the middle. (And don't forget to fry up those donut holes!) As for saving donuts for the next day or later in the week: Just don't. There's a reason day-old donuts cost 50 cents for a bag at a donut shop: They're terrible! Make these the day you need them. They will blow people's minds.

Create Your Epic

- ▼ The Hangover Breakfast Sandwich (page 102)
- ▼ Coffee and Donuts Shake (page 155)
- ▼ Captain Chow Donuts with Salty Peanut Butter Filling (page 180)

CHAPTER 4

THERE'S AN APP FOR THAT:
Nibbles and Passed Bites for the Crowd

MAC AND CHEESE PRETZEL BITES

This is the perfect little handheld delight for parties, "big game" gatherings, or movie night. Stuff 'em in your bag and take to the movie theater to enjoy at the latest new release! I need to start a website dedicated to hacking the movie theater–going experience … I got skills in that department, yo. I wouldn't take a dipping sauce, though; that's just messy. Besides, they have handy FREE mustard packets at movie theaters made just for these bites!

- 1 batch Pretzel Dough (page 60) proofed and ready to be turned out
- 3 cups Easy Creamy Shells and Cheese (page 16), chilled (see Tip)
- ½ cup (112 g) vegan butter, melted
- 2 teaspoons (5 g) garlic powder
- Fresh cracked pepper or ground black pepper
- Maldon or coarse sea salt

Suggested Sauce Pairings

- Beet Marinara (page 40)
- Blue Cheese Dressing (page 42)
- Red BBQ Sauce (page 48)

Preheat the oven to 425°F (220°C, or gas mark 7). Line 2 baking sheets with parchment paper.

Split the Pretzel Dough in half. Roll out the first half on a floured surface until it is ¼ inch (6 mm) thick. Using a 2½-inch (6-cm) cookie or biscuit cutter, create 22 rounds (gathering the scraps and rerolling the dough as needed). Repeat with the other half of the dough, creating 44 rounds total.

Add 1 level tablespoon (20 g) of shells and cheese to each round. Bring two sides into the middle, like a taco, and then fold in the other two sides, pressing all four sides together to enclose the macaroni and cheese in the dough round. Roll with the palms of your hands to create a smooth ball. Transfer to a prepared baking sheet; repeat with the remaining rounds and shells.

Whisk together the butter and garlic powder. Gently brush the tops of each bite with the butter mixture. Top with the pepper and salt. Bake for 14 to 16 minutes, or until the bites are golden brown.

Serve warm on a platter with a ramekin of dipping sauce on the side.

Yield: 10 to 12 servings

Tip

Make the version of the mac and cheese straight from the pot; no need to bake. But be sure to chill the shells completely so they're scoopable and stick together when constructing the bites. And hey, if you have any leftover Easy Creamy Shells and Cheese in the refrigerator, this is the perfect opportunity to use it!

DISCO PRETZEL BITES

It's time to up your appetizer game, and these pretzel bites impress every time! If you want the typical disco fries, follow this recipe and use the Crispy Drive-Thru Potato Wedges on page 26 instead of the pretzel bites. But I guarantee you, pretzel bites slathered in decadent gravy and robust mozzarella is the way to go! And the measurements here are just a guideline; if you want them gooier, have at it!

- ▼ 1 batch Pretzel Bites (page 60)
- ▼ 1 cup Mellow Mushroom Gravy (page 47), warmed
- ▼ ½ cup Saucy Mozzarella (page 45), warmed
- ▼ 2 scallions, roughly chopped

Divide the pretzel bites among 4 serving bowls and top each with ¼ cup (60 ml) gravy. Drizzle with 2 tablespoons (33 g) mozzarella and sprinkle with the scallions.

To serve as 1 larger presentation, pile all of the bites onto a large platter or large bowl. Slather with the gravy, drizzle with the mozzarella, and sprinkle with the scallions. Serve with a large serving spoon, or have your guests dig in, 1 pretzel bite at a time.

Yield: 4 servings

Tip

I like to serve extra gravy and mozzarella on the side if I have a guest that is feeling particularly saucy; they have the option to get their sauce on! If you've prepared everything in advance, reheat it all at once by placing the pretzel bites in an oven-safe skillet and topping with the gravy and mozzarella. Bake at 350°F (175°C, or gas mark 4) for 8 to 10 minutes, or until heated through.

CHILI CHEESE POTATO WEDGES WITH QUINOA BACON BITS

Ok, so maybe you are looking at this title thinking, "Whatever. It doesn't seem THAT epic." Oh, but my dear friend, truth sayin' time. These crispy wedges are paired with this robust cheese sauce and hearty downhome chili, and finished off with Quinoa Bacon Bits for that touch of smoky flavor you never knew you needed. Together they will bring you to your knees praising all things that are epic! You've been warned. Now go forth, make the most epic chili cheese concoction ever—I dare you.

- ▼ Crispy Drive-Thru Potato Wedges (page 26) or prepared store-bought frozen french fries
- ▼ 1 cup Mom's Chili (page 25) or store-bought vegan chili
- ▼ 1 cup The Cheesiest Cheese Sauce (page 44)
- ▼ 2 tablespoons Quinoa Bacon Bits (page 14)
- ▼ 1 scallion, roughly chopped

Divide the potato wedges between 2 plates. Add a layer of ½ cup chili over the wedges followed by a drizzle of ¼ to ½ cup cheese sauce. Sprinkle each serving with 1 tablespoon bacon bits, and top off both with the scallions.

Yield: 2 servings

Tip

Even though there are a few components to this dish, they're completely manageable. You'll want to make the wedges or fries fresh, but the cheese sauce and chili can be reheated from leftovers on the stovetop over medium-low heat. Still short for time? Don't stress; there's a quick fix to this recipe. You can build the same dish with store-bought frozen fries, vegan cheese sauce, and vegan chili. Chop up some store-bought vegan bacon to create bits, and finish off as directed with the scallion.

BREAKFAST NACHOS

Nachos are hands down one of my all-time favorite foods. For this book, it was important for me to include a version of nachos that I wish were a staple in American breakfasts; they're loaded with goodies and flavor! This is where some of my favorite recipes from the book (Eggsellent Eggs, The Cheesiest Cheese Sauce, and Avocado Sour Cream) come to play!

- 1 tablespoon (15 ml) olive oil
- ½ red bell pepper, roughly chopped
- 2 vegan sausage links, roughly chopped or crumbled
- 1 batch Eggsellent Eggs, scrambled (page 32)
- 1 cup The Cheesiest Cheese Sauce (page 44)
- 2 teaspoons (4 g) taco seasoning
- ½ cup (130 g) store-bought salsa
- ¼ cup (42 g) pineapple chunks, fresh or canned, roughly chopped
- Blue corn tortilla chips
- ½ cup (35 g) shredded red cabbage
- Avocado Sour Cream (page 50) or store-bought vegan sour cream
- 2 scallions, roughly chopped (optional)
- Micro greens (optional)

Heat the oil in a medium skillet over medium heat. Sauté the bell pepper and sausage for 2 to 4 minutes, or until the sausage is browned. Add the scramble. Mix until well combined and heated through, about 2 minutes, stirring frequently to avoid burning.

In a small saucepan over low heat, whisk together the cheese sauce with the taco seasoning for about 4 minutes, or until heated through.

In a small bowl, mix together the salsa and pineapple chunks.

To assemble the nachos: On a platter (I use my 12-inch [30-cm] pizza pan, but get bougie if you have a fancy platter), create the first layer of nachos with a single layer of tortilla chips. Top with half of the scramble, salsa, and cabbage. Drizzle with half of the cheese sauce, and add another layer of chips. Repeat with the remaining scramble, salsa, cabbage, and cheese sauce. Top with a generous dollop of sour cream in the center, and finish with a sprinkle of scallions and a pinch of micro greens, if using.

Yield: 6 to 8 servings

Tip

When I know I'm going to have guests for brunch, I like to prep all of the toppings the day before. Then I just have to reheat it all on the stovetop and build the nachos the next day for an easy and quick assembly! You can also split the recipe into smaller servings, if needed, dividing the toppings accordingly among 4 to 6 plates.

SWEET CHILI COCKTAIL PEANUTS

It used to be that I couldn't get enough cheese when I was at social functions; the cheese plate always called my name. Nowadays, my sights have shifted; if there's an array of mixed nuts, I'm going at them like a squirrel! These jazzed-up peanuts will keep both the squirrels and humans happy. (But, really, please don't actually give these to squirrels; I'm not sure that would be entirely safe!)

▼ Cooking spray

▼ 1½ cups (218 g) unsalted cocktail peanuts or unsalted peanuts

▼ ¼ cup (60 ml) agave

▼ 2 teaspoons (10 ml) chili garlic sauce

▼ ½ teaspoon garlic powder

▼ ½ teaspoon sea salt

Preheat the oven to 350°F (175°C, or gas mark 4). Line a baking sheet with parchment paper, and lightly coat it with cooking spray.

Spread the peanuts on the prepared baking sheet. Bake for 5 minutes. Remove from the oven and set aside.

In a small bowl, combine the agave, chili garlic sauce, garlic powder, and salt. Drizzle the mixture over the peanuts on the baking sheet and mix around with a spatula until all the peanuts are coated.

Return to the oven and bake for 5 minutes. Stir with a spatula and bake for an additional 5 minutes. Stir one last time and bake for another 5 minutes; the peanuts will be darker in color with some charred spots. Remove from the oven and cool for 10 minutes.

The peanuts will be a little sticky on the parchment paper. Slowly run a spatula under them, releasing them from the parchment. Peanuts will keep for 2 weeks in a sealed container.

Yield: 6 to 8 servings

Tip

My favorite brand of chili garlic sauce for this recipe is Huy Fong, but use whatever brand you like. Peanut allergy? No prob! Cashews are a great nut for this recipe but really, any nut (or even seed!) will do. Try pepitas mixed up with this sauce and baked for an out-of-this world salad topper. Warning: Since seeds are smaller, they need only about half the baking time, depending on the seed, so keep an eye on them.

Pictured:
Sweet Chili Cocktail Peanuts, Loxed and Loaded Bagel Bites, The Fancy Marga-Reba, Everything Buffalo Cauliflower Bites, Disco Pretzel Bites, Chili Cheese Potato Wedges with Quinoa Bacon Bits, and Jumbo Phish 'n Chips Sushi Roll

JUMBO PHISH 'N CHIPS SUSHI ROLL

My husband and I once took a private lesson with a master sushi chef for our anniversary, and we have memories that make us laugh to this day. Sushi is a super fun way to cook with other people, and it can be done with or without a sushi mat! When it comes to making sushi rolls, some people are naturals and some people take a little more practice. Just remember that no matter how it turns out aesthetically, it will be delicious!

- ◄ ¼ cup (60 ml) rice vinegar
- ◄ 2 tablespoons (26 g) organic cane sugar
- ◄ 1 teaspoon sea salt
- ◄ 4 cups (744 g) freshly cooked sushi rice
- ◄ 4 sheets nori
- ◄ 4 pieces Beer-Battered Tofu Phish (page 28), cut in half lengthwise
- ◄ 8 Crispy Drive-Thru Potato Wedges (page 26)
- ◄ ½ cup Fuss-Free Tartar Sauce (page 50)
- ◄ Sriracha hot sauce (optional)
- ◄ Chopped scallions (optional)

In a medium bowl, mix together the vinegar, sugar, and salt. Add the rice, and stir until all of the rice is coated with the vinegar mixture.

Prepare a small bowl of warm water and have it sitting nearby.

Lay a full nori sheet on a flat surface. Wet a hand and use that hand to spread 1 cup rice (186 g) over ¾ of the nori sheet, leaving 1½ inches (3.5 cm) at the top (the end farthest away from you) empty without rice.

In the middle of the rice, lay 2 strips of phish and 2 potato wedges crosswise (parallel with the bottom edge). Drizzle with 2 tablespoons (30 ml) tartar sauce. Dip your finger in the water and wet the edge of the nori sheet without the rice.

Pick up the bottom of the nori sheet, and carefully fold it over the filling. Pull the nori taut and use your fingers to keep the filling in place. Continue to roll up the sheet the rest of the way onto the wet edge; press down and hold 15 seconds to make sure the seam sticks.

With a very sharp knife, cut the roll into 6 pieces. Serve with the cut-side up, drizzled with Sriracha and sprinkled with scallions, if desired.

Yield: 4 servings (4 rolls, 24 pieces)

Tip

I love my bamboo sushi mat, and it has proven to be a worthwhile purchase. However, owning a sushi mat is a personal choice. If you don't have one and still don't feel comfortable free-styling it with these instructions, there are a bunch of fun videos on YouTube that will make you a sushi pro in no time. You can also try using parchment paper as a makeshift sushi mat.

LOXED AND LOADED BAGEL BITES

True story: I had never had bagels and lox until I went vegan! I used to wait tables at a place in Manhattan (a loooooong time ago), and one of the most popular brunch dishes was bagels and lox; I was always very confused, as I didn't see the appeal. Then I met the carrot lox, and I have been a fan ever since! The taste of the sea paired with luscious cream cheese, zesty red onions, and tangy capers is now a favorite of mine. One of the best vegan bagels and lox I've had is the Edith sandwich at Orchard Grocer in NYC, but when I'm home, I get my Loxed and Loaded groove on with this recipe.

For Carrot Lox:

- 2 carrots
- 1 tablespoon (15 ml) olive oil
- 1 teaspoon dulse flakes
- 1 teaspoon liquid smoke
- ¼ teaspoon sea salt
- ¼ teaspoon black pepper

For Bagel Bites:

- 36 bagel chips, pita chips, crackers, or homemade crostini (see Tip)
- ½ batch Dreamy Creamy Cream Cheese (page 41), with the scallion option
- ¼ cup (30 g) thinly sliced and chopped red onion
- 2 tablespoons (17 g) roughly chopped capers

To make the carrot lox: Use a vegetable peeler to peel the carrots into thin strips. Cut those strips into 1-inch (2.5-cm) pieces; set aside.

In a small container with a lid, mix together the olive oil, dulse, liquid smoke, salt, and pepper. Add the carrots, mix until they're well coated, cover, and refrigerate overnight to marinate.

To finish: Lay out the chips or crackers on a serving platter. Dollop each chip with 1 teaspoon cream cheese. Top with 2 or 3 pieces carrot lox, red onion, and capers.

Yield: 9 to 12 servings

Tip

Instead of bagel chips, make crostini by cutting a baguette into thin slices; drizzle with olive oil and toast in a skillet over medium heat until crisp on each side. Or forget about the finger-food version and live your best brunch life by using these components on a toasted bagel.

EVERYTHING BUFFALO CAULIFLOWER BITES

Cauliflower buffalo bites have swept the nation! Vegan restaurants and nonvegan restaurants alike serve them, and they are popular among patrons far and wide. I wanted to add a touch of EPIC to these with the "everything coating," but you should feel free to epic them up yourself—maybe by tossing them in the Sweet Thai Chili Sauce on page 46 or by serving them naked with the Coconut-Cheddar Fondue on page 43 on the side. Get creative!

For Buffalo Sauce:

- ▶ 1 cup (235 ml) hot sauce
- ▶ ¼ cup (55 g) vegan butter
- ▶ ¼ cup (60 g) packed organic dark brown sugar

For Everything Coating:

- ▶ 1 tablespoon (6 g) dried minced garlic
- ▶ 1 tablespoon (6 g) dried minced onion
- ▶ 2 teaspoons (6 g) black sesame seeds
- ▶ 2 teaspoons (12 g) Maldon or coarse sea salt

For Cauliflower Bites:

- ▶ 1 cup (125 g) all-purpose flour
- ▶ 1 cup (140 g) stone-ground yellow cornmeal or polenta
- ▶ ¼ cup (32 g) cornstarch
- ▶ 1 teaspoon sea salt
- ▶ ½ teaspoon black pepper
- ▶ 1½ cups (355 ml) seltzer water
- ▶ Canola oil or cooking spray
- ▶ 1 medium head cauliflower, trimmed and cut into bite-size florets
- ▶ 2 scallions, roughly chopped
- ▶ Blue Cheese Dressing (page 42), or store-bought vegan blue cheese dressing, for dipping

To make the buffalo sauce:

In a small saucepan, combine the hot sauce, butter, and brown sugar. Bring to a simmer over medium heat and cook for 2 to 4 minutes, or until the butter has melted and the sugar has dissolved. Remove from the heat and set aside.

To make the everything coating:

In a small bowl, combine the garlic, onion, sesame seeds, and salt. Set aside.

To make the cauliflower bites:

In a medium bowl, whisk together the flour, cornmeal, cornstarch, salt, and pepper. Slowly add the seltzer water, whisking until well combined and a thick batter has formed.

In a wok or large saucepan, pour 3 inches (7.5 cm) of canola oil. Heat the oil to 350°F (175°C) when tested with a candy thermometer or a drop of batter fries quickly and bubbles up to the top. Line a plate with paper towels.

Working in batches, transfer half of the cauliflower florets into the batter; mix around until all the florets are fully coated. Using tongs, pick up a piece of cauliflower, allowing excess batter to drip off, and carefully transfer into the frying oil; repeat with the remaining battered pieces.

Fry in small batches for 4 to 6 minutes, or until golden brown. Use a slotted spoon to transfer the cauliflower to the paper towel–lined plate. Repeat until all of the cauliflower is fried.

In a large bowl, toss ¼ of the fried cauliflower bites with ¼ of the buffalo sauce and 2 teaspoons (10 ml) of the "everything" mixture (you get a more even coating if you do it in batches). Transfer the bites to a serving tray and repeat for the remaining bites. Sprinkle the plated cauliflower with any remaining everything coating and the scallions, if using.

Serve with Blue Cheese Dressing on the side, for dipping.

Baked option: If you prefer to stay away from frying, coat the cauliflower with the batter as directed, making sure to remove as much excess batter as possible. Transfer to a parchment-lined baking sheet lightly coated with cooking spray, and bake at 450°F (230°C, or gas mark 8) for 30 minutes, flipping once, or until lightly browned. Remove from the oven and continue with the recipe as directed.

Yield: 6 to 8 servings

Tip

Want a meatier texture? Make these with the Simply Seitan on page 22 by cutting the seitan into bite-size pieces and using in place of the cauliflower. If you ran out of batter before you coated all the cauliflower, store the leftover cauliflower in the fridge for use in Savory Cheddar Fondue Waffle Bowl on page 139.

CHAPTER 5

MONSTER HANDHELDS:
Beastly Bites Fit for Kings and Queens

TRIPLE-DECKER BREKKY SAMMY

Let's face it: The world is in love with breakfast sandwiches, and this is the mother of them all. The idea that you can put some breakfast staples like sausage and eggs on a sandwich and be all set is genius! Breakfast sandwiches have been kicking around for generations, with the first sighting of one in an American cookbook in 1897. But this isn't your standard breakfast fare. Let's add another level here for a triple-decker sandwich to beat all breakfast sandwiches. Eat your heart out, 1897! And hey, cut yourself some slack and take these elements one step at a time: Make the eggs, hash browns, or sausages a day before and then simply reheat at 250°F (120°C, or gas mark ½) for 10 minutes while you whip up the rest the next day. Plan ahead, and Martha Stewart this beast for a stress-free sandwich build—*it's a good thing.*

- 4 Breakfast Sausage Patties (page 18), or store-bought vegan breakfast patties, cooked

- 8 pieces Eggsellent Eggs, baked (page 32)

- 4 slices vegan American cheese or vegan cheese of choice

- 6 vegan English muffins, toasted

- ¼ cup (60 g) ketchup

- ¼ cup Hollandaise for Days (page 40)

- 8 Happy Hash Browns (page 15), or store-bought hash brown patties

- 1 avocado, peeled and sliced (see Tip)

Warm a large skillet with a lid over medium heat until it's hot. Set 2 sausage patties in the skillet and top each with 2 pieces of egg and 1 slice of cheese. Add 1 tablespoon (15 ml) water to the skillet and immediately cover for 20 to 30 seconds, or until the cheese melts. Remove the sausage stacks from the skillet and repeat with the remaining patties, eggs, and cheese. Vegan cheese can be tricky to melt sometimes, and this is a quick hack to have a surefire perfect melt.

Starting with the bottom half of an English muffin, spread with 1 tablespoon (15 g) of ketchup and top with a sausage stack. Add another muffin half ("cranny" or cut-side up) and spread with 1 tablespoon (15 ml) hollandaise. Top with 2 hash brown patties, ¼ of the avocado, and finish with the top half of the muffin. Repeat with the remaining ingredients.

Yield: 4 servings

Tip

To peel and slice an avocado, use a sharp knife to cut the avocado in half, rotating around the seed lengthwise with the knife. Remove the seed by either slipping a spoon between the seed and the fruit and wiggling it out, or by aiming the knife at the seed and whacking it, using just enough force to get the knife to stick into the seed, and then twist it out. Cut the avocado into 4 sections and peel off the skin; then cut the 4 sections into slices and gently press down to fan out the slices.

BACON MACARONI AND CHEESE BBQ BLUE BURGER

You don't have to go to a silly chain restaurant to have a burger that's taller than your pint of beer; I've got you covered! Don't be discouraged by the make-ahead items in this recipe; I encourage you to go for it and make them all from scratch because it's super rewarding. Make the Easy Creamy Shells and Cheese for dinner one night, then use the leftovers for this sandwich to get the most use of the Mac recipe (and also be prepared)! I also applaud you if you want to go out and buy items at the store—there's no shame in that game. The end result is just as enjoyable, no matter if you build it from the ground up or rely on some ready-made vegan products.

- ▼ 2 cups Easy Creamy Shells and Cheese (page 16), or store-bought boxed vegan macaroni and cheese, hot
- ▼ ½ cup Quinoa Bacon Bits (page 14)
- ▼ 1 cup (55 g) roughly chopped romaine lettuce
- ▼ 8 vegan hamburger bun bottoms, toasted (see Tip, page 94)
- ▼ 4 All-American Burgers (page 18), or store-bought vegan burgers, cooked
- ▼ ¼ cup Blue Cheese Dressing (page 42) or store-bought vegan blue cheese dressing
- ▼ 8 slices tomato
- ▼ 8 slices red onion
- ▼ 8 strips vegan bacon, cooked (optional)
- ▼ 12 pickle chips
- ▼ ¼ cup Red BBQ Sauce (page 48), or store-bought BBQ sauce
- ▼ 4 vegan hamburger bun tops, toasted

In a medium bowl, combine the shells and cheese with the bacon bits until the bacon is well distributed; set aside.

Place ¼ cup (about 14 g) lettuce on a bottom bun, top with 1 burger, ¼ of the blue cheese, 2 slices tomato, and 2 slices onion. Top with a second bottom bun and add 2 strips bacon (if using) and 3 pickle chips. Top with ½ cup (110 g) shells mixture and 1 tablespoon (15 ml) BBQ sauce, followed by a top bun. For an epic presentation, plunge a steak knife into the middle of the burger.

Yield: 4 servings

Tip

There are vegan macaroni and cheese brands available for purchase in stores these days, which make it so much easier to tackle this recipe epic style. Take it a step further and purchase your burgers from a store as well and you are halfway to epic already! To make some quick strips of veggie bacon at home, use a vegetable peeler to create thin strips of carrot. Fry them in a little oil over medium heat in a skillet until desired doneness. The sides will get dark and curl up like bacon. Sprinkle with some smoked sea salt for that extra touch!

LOBSTER ROLL 'N A BISCUIT SLIDERS

These biscuits though, am I right?! If you've ever dined at Red Lobster and had a bite of those Cheddar-Bay Biscuits and couldn't resist a second helping, have I got a treat for you: those biscuits, piled high with lobster roll filling. I wasn't a fan of lobster rolls as a nonvegan, but when I created them for this book, I fell in love. If you're making both components from scratch, get the biscuits in the oven before making the lobster roll filling.

▶ 1 batch Garlicky Cheddar Biscuits (page 68), baked

▶ 1 batch Lobster Rolls filling (page 24)

Cut each biscuit in half so there is a top and a bottom. Place ¼ cup (68 g) Lobster Rolls filling on the bottom half, and set the top half of the biscuit on top.

Yield: 6 servings (12 sliders)

Tip

These are fun to pass at Fourth of July parties! Stick little American flags in them for a festive touch.

BACON–CINNAMON ROLL BURGER WITH PEANUT BUTTER ▶

Full disclosure, this burger came about because I was trying to design one more over-the-top, strange and crazy concoction to put in this chapter. Truth be told, it's so freaking delicious! I surprised even myself with it. The test kitchen picture got like upon like on Instagram, so be sure to post a pic of your creation on your social media feeds so people can "ooh" and "ahh" over it. And tag me *@theveganroadie* so I can see the goodness too!

▶ 4 Cinnadiction Rolls, bacon variation (page 66)

▶ 4 All-American Burgers (page 18) or store-bought vegan burgers, cooked

▶ ½ cup (130 g) creamy peanut butter

If the rolls are freshly made, wait until they have cooled completely and are easily handled. Cut them in half to create a top and bottom "bun," with the iced side as the top bun.

Place a burger on the bottom bun and slather it with 2 tablespoons (32 g) peanut butter; top with the top bun.

Yield: 4 servings

Tip

This bad boy actually holds up as a handheld, though messy, and it's super fun to eat! But if you're wearing a new shirt or don't have a bib on hand, I suggest using a knife and fork, and serve it with wet naps to tidy up after!

BREAKFAST PLATTER DOG

I can't take credit for this delight; credit goes to Keaton Tucker of Cycle Dogs in Seattle. Keaton is a true original, creating genuine vegan dogs for the masses. You can see more about him and the awesome work he is doing in the Seattle episode of *The Vegan Roadie*. But for starters, get a taste of Cycle Dogs with this treat, no matter where you hang your hat! It's like your favorite diner's giant breakfast platter—in a bun. And, what's that? A little bird just told me you can make the scramble the day before and simply reheat it when mixing with the veggies here to ease the build on this bad boy. Thanks, little birdie!

- ▼ ¼ cup (60 g) vegan mayonnaise
- ▼ 2 tablespoons (30 ml) Sriracha hot sauce
- ▼ 1 tablespoon (15 ml) olive oil
- ▼ 1 onion, thinly sliced
- ▼ 1 red bell pepper, roughly chopped
- ▼ 2 vegan sausage links, crumbled or chopped (optional)
- ▼ 1 batch Eggsellent Eggs, scrambled (page 32)
- ▼ 4 vegan sandwich rolls or hot dog buns, toasted (see Tip)
- ▼ 8 Happy Hash Browns (page 15), halved, or store-bought hash brown patties
- ▼ 4 vegan hot dogs, cooked
- ▼ 2 scallions, chopped

In a small bowl, whisk together the mayonnaise and Sriracha; set aside.

Heat the olive oil in a large skillet over medium heat. Add the onion, bell pepper, and sausage (if using). Sauté for about 4 minutes, until the vegetables are soft and the sausage is browned. Add the scramble. Mix until well combined and heated through, about 2 minutes, stirring frequently to avoid burning.

Set an open bun on a plate and place 2 halves of the hash browns on each side. Place a hot dog in the middle, topped with ¼ of the scramble mixture, followed by a drizzle of the mayonnaise mixture. Finish off the hot dog with a sprinkle of scallions.

Repeat with the remaining ingredients.

Yield: 4 servings

Tip

To toast your buns, lightly butter the insides and tops with vegan butter. Gently open up the bun and press face down on a hot skillet. If the bun is fragile and you fear it might break if opened all the way, just toast the outside tops; it still adds a nice layer of crunch and flavor.

WAFFLE TOT GRILLED CHEESE

What the WHAT!? Yes, an ooey-gooey delectable grilled cheese sandwich housed between crisp tater tots in the form of a waffle … dreams do come true! Honestly, I love to dip my grilled cheese sandwiches in tomato soup, and one day I was lazy and dipped it in ketchup, which then got me thinking, "What if the crust were made of potatoes!?" And with that thought, the Waffle Tot Grilled Cheese was born.

▾ Cooking spray

▾ 4 cups tater tots (about ½ of a 32-ounce or 907 g bag), thawed at room temperature for 30 minutes

▾ ½ cup (60 g) vegan mozzarella shreds

▾ ½ cup (58 g) vegan cheddar shreds

▾ 1 tablespoon (5 g) nutritional yeast

▾ Ketchup, for dipping

The tots may overflow the sides of the waffle iron. To avoid a mess, place parchment paper or a baking sheet under the iron for easy cleanup.

Preheat the iron according to the manufacturer's instructions. Lightly coat with cooking spray and layer the bottom with 2 cups (227 g) of the tots. Close the iron and cook for 2 minutes, or just until the tots take the shape of the iron.

Sprinkle the mozzarella, cheddar, and nutritional yeast evenly over the waffle, then top with the remaining tots. Close the iron as much as it will close, and let sit for 2 minutes. Place a towel on top (use a thick towel or one folded several times to protect your hands from the heat) and slowly press the top down to flatten the waffle. Cook another 2 minutes. Using the towel again, press and hold the iron down one last time as far as it can go down; holding it in place, cook for 2 minutes. Remove your hands, and let cook an additional 2 minutes, or until the crust is golden brown and crispy.

Turn off the waffle iron and raise the top. Let the sandwich cool for a few minutes, then pop it out of the iron with a fork and transfer to a cutting board. Cut the sandwich into 4 pieces and serve with ketchup for dipping.

Yield: 2 to 4 servings

Tip

Use those overflowing bits of cheese and tater tots that come out of the sides of the waffle iron and mix them into the scrambled Eggsellent Eggs on page 32 for a breakfast treat!

SWEET THAI PEANUT CAULIFLOWER TACOS

Meatless Mondays aren't just for Mondays anymore, and Taco Tuesdays are certainly not just meant for Tuesdays! Enjoy these meatless tacos any day of the week; the combination of savory and sweet paired with crispy cauliflower is also a win-win at any party. This is my husband, David's, absolute favorite recipe in the book, and he has tried them all!

For Sauce:

- ▼ 1 batch Sweet Thai Chili Sauce (page 46)
- ▼ ¼ cup (65 g) creamy peanut butter (see Tip, page 182; same peanut butter rules apply)

For Cauliflower:

- ▼ Canola oil
- ▼ 1 cup (125 g) all-purpose flour
- ▼ 1 cup (140 g) stone-ground yellow cornmeal or polenta
- ▼ ¼ cup (32 g) cornstarch
- ▼ 1 teaspoon sea salt
- ▼ ½ teaspoon black pepper
- ▼ 1½ cups (355 ml) seltzer water
- ▼ 1 head cauliflower, cut into tiny florets (see Tip)

For Tacos:

- ▼ 8 small (6-inch/15-cm) soft taco shells, warmed (see Tip)
- ▼ 1 cup (110 g) shredded carrots
- ▼ 1 cup (70 g) shredded red cabbage
- ▼ 2 scallions, chopped (optional)
- ▼ Sweet Chili Cocktail Peanuts (page 80) or plain cocktail peanuts, crushed (optional)
- ▼ White sesame seeds (optional)

To make the sauce: In a small saucepan whisk together the Thai chili sauce and peanut butter. Bring to a simmer and heat for 2 to 5 minutes, or until all the peanut butter has mixed in and the sauce is smooth and creamy. Remove from the heat and set aside.

To make the cauliflower:

In a wok or large saucepan, pour 3 inches (7.5 cm) of canola oil. Heat the oil 350°F (175°C) when tested with a candy thermometer or a drop of batter bubbles up to the top and fries quickly. Line a plate with paper towels.

In a medium bowl, whisk together the flour, cornmeal or polenta, cornstarch, salt, and pepper. Slowly whisk in the seltzer water until well combined and a thick batter forms.

Working in 2 batches, transfer half of the cauliflower florets to the batter. Mix around until all the pieces are fully coated. Using tongs, shake off excess batter and carefully transfer battered cauliflower pieces, 1 at a time, into the frying oil.

Fry in small batches for 4 to 6 minutes, or until golden brown. Use a slotted spoon to transfer the cauliflower to the paper towel–lined plate. Repeat with the remaining cauliflower.

When all the cauliflower has been fried, transfer it to a large bowl and toss with the peanut-chili sauce.

To build the tacos: Start with a warm tortilla, 2 tablespoons (about 14 g) carrot, 2 tablespoons (about 9 g) cabbage, 6 to 8 coated cauliflower florets, and a sprinkle of scallions, peanuts, and sesame seeds (if using). Serve warm.

Yield: 4 servings

Tip

It's important for these florets to be small so that several can fit on a taco. To make them the size of 1 or 2 marbles, completely remove the stem and cut the floret into smaller florets. Before you fry the cauliflower, warm the taco shells by setting them on a baking sheet (overlapping is okay) and placing in 200°F (93°C, or gas mark ½) oven until time to build the tacos.

NORITOS LOS TACOS

While complaints abounded when a certain "Mexican" fast food chain was busted for serving "mystery meat" in 2011, consumers continued to buy tacos—and more—after the mystery ingredient was revealed to be simply… oats. Doesn't seem so awful, right? The secret ingredient might actually be the safest ingredient in the mystery meat, come to think of it. I didn't end up with oats in this recipe, but instead some flour to get the same sort of "creamy effect" of the mystery meat. This recipe is a plant-based replica of a certain stunt taco combining that mystery meat and a popular brand of chips—but the mystery is solved here!

For Mystery Meat:

▼ 2 tablespoons (30 ml) olive oil

▼ 1 package (10 to 13 ounces, or 280 to 369 g) frozen vegan beef crumbles

▼ 1 tablespoon (8 g) chili powder

▼ 1 teaspoon dried minced onion

▼ ½ teaspoon sea salt

▼ ½ teaspoon paprika

▼ ½ teaspoon garlic powder

▼ ¼ cup (32 g) all-purpose flour

▼ ½ cup (120 ml) water

For Noritos Shells:

▼ 1 packet (1 to 1.25 ounces/28 to 35 g) taco seasoning

▼ 2 tablespoons (10 g) nutritional yeast

▼ Cooking spray

▼ 12 hard taco shells

For Tacos:

▼ Shredded lettuce

▼ Diced tomatoes or chunky salsa

▼ Avocado Sour Cream (page 50), or store-bought vegan sour cream (optional)

▼ Shredded vegan cheddar shreds

To make the mystery meat:

Heat the olive oil in a large skillet over medium heat. Add the frozen beef crumbles and cook for 4 to 6 minutes, or until browned. Add the chili powder, dried onion, salt, paprika, and garlic powder, stirring until well combined. Add the flour and stir until the meat is coated. Add the water and cook for 2 to 4 minutes, stirring frequently, until the mixture thickens slightly and starts to bubble. If the mixture doesn't have a creamy texture, add ¼ to ½ cup (60 to 120 ml) more water, as needed. Cover and remove from the heat.

To make the Noritos shells:

Preheat the oven to 375°F (190°C, or gas mark 5). Line a baking sheet with parchment paper.

In a high-speed blender or food processor, pulse the taco seasoning and nutritional yeast into a fine powder; transfer to a plate.

Spray the outside of a taco shell with cooking spray, coating the entire outside. Dip each side into the seasoning mixture, sprinkling and patting the seasoning onto any empty spots. Lightly tap the shell on the plate to remove any excess seasoning. Set on the prepared baking sheet. Repeat with the remaining shells.

Bake for 4 minutes, or until slightly darker in color. Remove from the oven, and let the shells cool until easily handled.

To build the tacos: In a taco shell, start with a layer of meat and top it with lettuce, tomatoes or salsa, sour cream (if using), and cheese.

Yield: 4 to 6 servings

Tip

Make this a taco party! Make the meat and shells as directed and set out more toppings such as guacamole, a variety of salsas, chopped scallions, and chopped red cabbage. Let your family and friends build their own tacos.

FRIED CHICKEN 'N WAFFLE BENEDICT SANDWICH

Chicken 'n waffles have been a beloved classic for years, but this ain't your average Southern-inspired plate. The combination here of crispy chicken with egg and the traditional hollandaise sandwiched between a fluffy and crispy sweet potato waffle is worth getting out of bed for. Make the chicken and egg ahead of time and reheat on a baking sheet in the oven at 250°F (120°C, or gas mark ½) while you whip up the waffles. Then build that sandwich, slather it in delicious hollandaise sauce, and serve extra on the side for dipping!

- ▶ 3 Sweet Potato Waffles (page 70), 12 pieces separated into triangles or squares

- ▶ 1½ cups (78 g) baby spinach

- ▶ 6 pieces Fried Chicken, cutlet size (see recipe and Tip on page 23)

- ▶ 1 batch Eggsellent Egg, baked (page 32)

- ▶ ½ cup Hollandaise for Days (page 40), plus more for dipping

Build the sandwich by placing a small bed of about 6 to 8 leaves of baby spinach on a piece of waffle. Top the spinach with a piece of hot fried chicken followed by 2 pieces of egg and a heaping tablespoon (about 15 to 20 ml) of hollandaise. Top with another piece of waffle, and insert a sandwich pick into the center.

Repeat with remaining ingredients. Serve while still warm.

Yield: 6 sandwiches

Tip

Make that hollandaise ahead so you can just pull it out of the refrigerator when you are building these beauties. People LOVE benedict-y things on social media so be sure to make all of your friends jealous with pictures and tag me @theveganroadie, or just invite me over for brunch!

HUSHPUPPY PHISH FILLET SANDWICH

I didn't frequent fast food fish restaurants before I went vegan, but when I did pay a visit to one chain in particular, I could shovel their scrumptious hushpuppies down my food trap like I was trying to win a contest! This sandwich is a combo of the popular fish fillet sandwich and the beloved hushpuppy patty. Enjoy them together, but there's no shame in a simple hushpuppy sandwich either! To keep everything warm and crispy, make the hushpuppies first and place in a 200°F (93°C, or gas mark ½) oven while you work on the phish, then build that sandwich to epic heights!

For Hushpuppy Patties:

- 1 can (15 ounces/426 g) chickpeas, drained and rinsed

- ¾ cup (105 g) stone-ground cornmeal or polenta

- ½ cup (64 g) all-purpose flour

- ½ cup (80 g) minced onion

- 6 tablespoons (90 ml) unsweetened soy or almond milk

- 2 cloves garlic, minced

- 2 teaspoons (9 g) baking powder

- 1 teaspoon sea salt

- Canola oil

For Sandwich:

- 4 vegan sesame-topped hamburger buns, toasted (see Tip, page 94)

- 2 cups Murphy's Slaw (page 27)

- ¼ cup (60 g) ketchup

- 8 pieces Beer-Battered Tofu Phish (page 28)

- ¼ cup Fuss-Free Tartar Sauce (page 50)

- Micro greens or arugula

To make the hushpuppies:

In a large bowl, mash the chickpeas with a fork or potato masher. Add the cornmeal, flour, onion, milk, garlic, baking powder, and salt; mix until well combined. Divide the mixture into 4 parts and form each part into a patty, about the size of a burger. Set aside.

In a heavy skillet, pour about 2 inches (5 cm) of canola oil. Heat the oil to 350°F (175°C) when tested with a candy thermometer or until bubbles form around the handle of a wooden spoon when inserted into the oil. Line a plate with paper towels.

Use a slotted spatula to gently transfer the patties into the hot oil; fry 1 or 2 at a time depending on the size of your skillet. Fry for 2 to 4 minutes, or until golden brown and cooked through. Remove from the oil to the paper towel–lined plate.

To make the sandwich: Top a bottom bun with ½ cup (53 g) slaw and then a hushpuppy patty. Top the patty with 1 tablespoon (15 g) ketchup, 2 pieces phish, and 1 tablespoon (15 ml) tartar sauce. Finish it off with a fistful of micro greens or arugula, and then add the top bun. Repeat with the remaining ingredients.

Yield: 4 servings

Tip

You can make a more healthful version of the hushpuppy patties by baking them on a parchment-lined baking sheet at 425°F (220°C, or gas mark 7) for 18 minutes, flipping once, until golden brown. Don't forget to save the aquafaba (liquid) from the can of chickpeas to use in Easy Whip 2 Ways (page 53)!

THE HANGOVER BREAKFAST SANDWICH

This sandwich can go one of two ways: Either a poor hungover soul will be presented with it, get very excited, and devour it instantly, OR, the sight of this combination might put said soul over the edge and send them straight back to bed to sleep it off. Hangovers can be so tricky, eh? Good news! You don't have to be hungover to enjoy this masterpiece, but if you are, it might temporarily help you feel a little better. Planned ahead? Look at you! Just warm the sausage and eggs in a 200°F (93°C, or gas mark ½) oven for 10 minutes before melting the cheese on them. And this is the ONE time I will suggest a day-old donut, only because I don't trust you to make donuts from scratch hungover, and it actually helps give the bun a bit more of a stable structure too!

- 6 Crispy Cream Donuts with traditional glaze (page 71)

- 6 Breakfast Sausage Patties (page 18), or store-bought vegan sausage patties, cooked

- 1 batch Eggsellent Eggs, baked (page 32), cut into 12 pieces

- 6 slices vegan American cheese or vegan cheese slices of choice

Cut the donuts in half like hamburger buns so there is a top and bottom half; set aside.

Warm a large skillet with a lid over medium heat until it's hot. Set 2 sausage patties in the skillet and top each with 2 pieces of egg and 1 slice of cheese. Pour 1 tablespoon (15 ml) water into the skillet and immediately cover for 20 to 30 seconds, or until the cheese melts. Vegan cheese can be tricky to melt sometimes; this is a quick hack to have a surefire perfect melt.

Remove the sausage stacks from the skillet and place one each on a bottom donut bun; finish by adding the top donut bun. Repeat with the remaining ingredients.

Yield: 6 servings

Tip

Use any vegan donut you want for this! I know some people are lucky enough to have vegan donut options in their hometowns. If that's you and you want to skip making donuts from scratch, pick some up and get your breakfast sandwich game on point.

MAC DADDY CRUNCH BURRITO

I once had a "freeto" burrito from a food trailer in Austin called the Vegan Yacht. I loved it so much—as much as I used to love Big Macs—that I decided to put the two favorite junk foods together. I highly recommend a visit to as many food trailers as you can if you visit Austin; it's their thing—and for good reason. (Special shout-out to Arlo's food truck for the best vegan double bacon cheeseburger you will ever—EVER—have!)

- ▶ 1 batch Fuss-Free Tartar Sauce (page 50)
- ▶ 1 tablespoon (11 g) yellow mustard
- ▶ 1 tablespoon (15 g) ketchup
- ▶ 4 large (10-inch/25-cm) flour tortillas
- ▶ ½ cup (80 g) thinly sliced onion
- ▶ 2 cups (110 g) roughly chopped romaine lettuce
- ▶ 4 All-American Burgers (page 18), or 4 store-bought vegan burgers, cooked and cut into ½-inch (1-cm) pieces
- ▶ ½ cup (75 g) cherry tomatoes, halved
- ▶ 1 cup (115 g) vegan cheddar shreds
- ▶ 2 cups (124 g) Fritos or crushed tortilla chips

In a small bowl, combine the Tartar Sauce, mustard, and ketchup.

Lay a tortilla on a flat surface and start building the burrito as follows: 2 tablespoons (30 ml) Tartar Sauce mixture spread across the center of the tortilla, 2 tablespoons (20 g) onion, ½ cup (about 28 g) lettuce, ¼ of the vegan patty pieces (1 burger), 2 tablespoons (19 g) tomatoes, ¼ cup (29 g) cheese, and ¼ cup (16 g) Fritos.

Fold the part of the tortilla closest to you over the filling, tucking it in tightly under the filling if possible. Fold both sides in and roll the burrito up and away from you while keeping the sides tucked in. Sometimes this takes some practice; a tight roll ensures the ingredients will stay put and not fall out when cutting in half or taking a bite.

Repeat with the remaining ingredients. Cut in half before serving.

Yield: 4 servings

Tip

If you can find larger burrito tortillas, I say go for it! I'm only ever lucky enough to find the 10-inch (25-cm) in the grocery store, but the larger, the better to really get a grip on wrapping it up nicely.

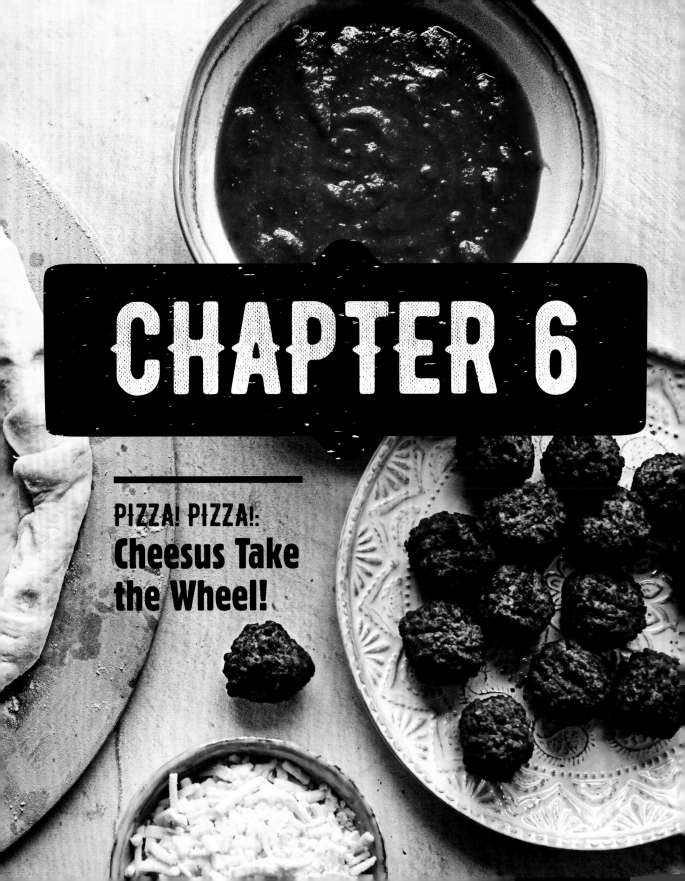

CHAPTER 6

PIZZA! PIZZA!:
Cheesus Take the Wheel!

DEEP-DISH BRUNCH PIZZA

I love biscuits and gravy, and I also love pizza. The world needs a recipe that offers both in epic proportions. This deep-dish pizza satisfies the crowd, one slice at a time. Layered on a cheesy garlic biscuit crust and topped with a savory and robust sausage gravy and a hearty scramble with melted cheese, it's a brunch lover's paradise.

- ▶ Cooking spray
- ▶ Cornmeal or flour
- ▶ 1 batch Garlicky Cheddar Biscuits dough (page 68)
- ▶ 1 tablespoon (15 ml) olive oil
- ▶ ½ red onion, diced
- ▶ ½ green bell pepper, diced
- ▶ 1 cup (70 g) stemmed and sliced baby bella or white button mushrooms
- ▶ 1 batch Eggsellent Eggs, scrambled (page 32)
- ▶ 1 cup Sausage Gravy (page 68)
- ▶ ¼ to ½ cup (30 to 58 g) vegan cheddar shreds
- ▶ Sriracha hot sauce (optional)
- ▶ Chopped fresh parsley or chives (optional)

Preheat the oven to 450°F (230°C, or gas mark 8). Lightly coat a 9-inch (23-cm) springform pan or round cake pan with cooking spray.

Dust the greased pan with cornmeal or flour. Spread the dough into the pan and push it out to the sides, creating a wall around the edges at least 1½ inches (3.5 cm) high. Bake the crust for 12 minutes and remove from the oven.

While the crust is baking, heat the olive oil in a large skillet over medium heat. Add the onion, bell pepper, and mushrooms. Sauté for 3 to 5 minutes, or until the vegetables have softened and the mushrooms have wilted. Add the scramble. Mix until well combined and heated through, about 2 minutes, stirring frequently to avoid burning; remove from the heat and set aside.

Using the bottom of a ladle, press down on the center of the baked crust to push the crust down and create more room for toppings. Press down at least an inch or more—as much as you can— being mindful not to crush the sides.

Use the ladle to spoon the gravy into the center. Top with the scramble mixture and sprinkle with desired amount of cheese. Bake for 14 to 16 minutes, or until the top is just starting to brown.

Remove from the oven and cool at least 10 minutes before removing the side of the springform pan (if using). Drizzle with Sriracha and sprinkle with parsley or chives, if desired. Slice into 8 pieces and serve warm.

Yield: 8 servings

Tip

There are a lot of scratch-made items in this recipe to get to the epic finish line—I'm totally aware! But I promise you it is worth it. Make the scramble and gravy the day before to be an extra preppy Polly; just be sure to reheat them over low heat before piling them on the pizza. Or be a hero the day of: Make the dough and gravy first and tackle the scramble while the crust does its first bake. Or stop listening to me—you chose this recipe, you might have a plan of attack already! Go with your gut.

PIZZABON

As I've mentioned, I will eat pizza in any form, and this is one of my favorites! After I created the Cinnadiction Rolls (page 66), I was obsessed with using that dough as a blank canvas for some of my favorite things. This Pizzabon is fluffy and full of zesty and robust flavor, thanks to the marinara topped with the Saucy Mozzarella from page 45. You'll be holding yourself back from seconds!

- ▼ Canola oil or cooking spray
- ▼ 1 batch Cinnadiction Rolls dough (page 66), proofed and ready to be turned out
- ▼ 1 cup (250 g) store-bought marinara sauce
- ▼ 1 cup (115 g) vegan mozzarella shreds
- ▼ 2 tablespoons (10 g) nutritional yeast
- ▼ 2 tablespoons (6 g) Italian seasoning
- ▼ ¼ to ½ cup Saucy Mozzarella (page 45)
- ▼ Hemp Parmesan (page 14) or store-bought vegan parmesan
- ▼ Roughly chopped fresh basil

Lightly coat a 9 x 13-inch (23 x 33-cm) baking dish with canola oil or cooking spray.

On a floured surface, roll out the dough until it is a 16 x 12-inch (39 x 30-cm) rectangle, about ¼ inch (6 mm) thick, with the long edge toward you.

Spread the marinara evenly over the surface of the dough. Sprinkle with the mozzarella shreds, nutritional yeast, and Italian seasoning. Roll up the dough from the bottom to the top as tightly and evenly as possible; set it on its seam. Cut the dough into 12 equal pieces, about 1½ inches (3.5 cm) thick.

Place the rolls, cut-sides up, into the prepared dish. There should be 4 rows with 3 rolls in each, with some space between each roll. Cover with a clean kitchen towel and let rest in a warm place for 25 to 30 minutes, or until they have risen and expanded. While they are rising, preheat the oven to 350°F (175°C, or gas mark 4).

Bake for 35 to 40 minutes, or until the tops are lightly browned. Cool in the dish for 10 minutes.

Drizzle the desired amount of Saucy Mozzarella over the rolls and sprinkle with the parmesan and basil.

Yield: 12 servings

Tip

Add your favorite pizza toppings into the mix! Cut your favorite vegetables and vegan meats into small pieces, lightly sauté, then evenly disperse them over the dough on top of the marinara filling before rolling it up for an extra-epic pizza bun.

FRANKS 'N MAC PIZZA

I have seen many a pizza piled high with macaroni and cheese in my day, but I wanted to take it one step further! For the kid in me (and also in you), I offer up the Franks 'n Mac Pizza, huzzah! Full of those things you loved as a kid—hot dogs AND macaroni and cheese—with a crispy crust to make it a food you can eat with your hands; it's a win-win. I like a rectangle pan for this pizza, but if you prefer a traditional round pan, the pizza will be just as scrumptious!

- 1 batch Pizza Dough (page 57), divided, enough for 1 pizza (see Tip on page 57)
- Olive oil
- 2 cups Easy Creamy Shells and Cheese (page 16)
- 2 vegan hot dogs, sliced
- ¼ cup Saucy Mozzarella (page 45) or vegan mozzarella shreds
- Ketchup (optional)
- Sriracha hot sauce (optional)
- Chopped fresh parsley

Preheat the oven to 450°F (230°C, or gas mark 8). Line a 9 x 13-inch (23 x 33-cm) baking sheet with parchment paper.

On a lightly floured surface, stretch out or roll the Pizza Dough into a large rectangle. Fit it into the baking sheet and brush lightly with olive oil over the entire dough. Bake for 6 minutes, or until it is just starting to brown slightly and rise.

Meanwhile, in a medium bowl, combine the shells and cheese with the hot dogs until the hot dogs are evenly distributed.

Remove the pizza crust from the oven and spread the pasta mixture evenly over the top. Top with the mozzarella, and bake for an additional 12 to 14 minutes, or until the tops of the shells are just starting to brown.

Remove from the oven, and drizzle with ketchup and Sriracha (if using) and sprinkle with fresh parsley. Cool for 5 to 10 minutes before slicing into 8 pieces. Serve hot.

Yield: 4 to 8 servings

Tip

Combine the ketchup and Sriracha in a small bowl to create a spicy ketchup, so you only have to drizzle one condiment over the top. You can also use this new spicy creation on burgers or to dip Crispy Drive-Thru Potato Wedges (page 26)!

PIZZA BURRITO SUPREME

The best part about a burrito is that the tortilla is like a plate you can eat with all your favorite flavors rolled up into it! When I thought of it that way, I couldn't help but turn pizza into a burrito as well. This is an awesome recipe to serve up on game day to make all your vegan (and nonvegan) friends "ooooh" and "ahhhh" at your mad culinary skills. You can cut it into smaller pieces for an appetizer, or take this bad boy on when secret-eating your feelings. I mean, if that is something you do with pizza … I've never done that, I've just heard it's something people do.

- ▼ 1 batch Pizza Dough (page 57), divided, enough for 1 pizza (see Tip on page 57)

- ▼ 2 tablespoons (30 ml) olive oil, divided

- ▼ 1 cup Beet Marinara (page 40), or store-bought marinara

- ▼ 1 cup (115 g) vegan mozzarella shreds, divided

- ▼ ½ green bell pepper, chopped

- ▼ ½ red onion, chopped

- ▼ ½ cup (88 g) stemmed, sliced, and chopped baby bella mushrooms

- ▼ 1 vegan sausage link, thinly sliced

- ▼ 1 can (2.25 ounces/64 g) sliced black olives, drained

- ▼ Blue Cheese Dressing (page 42), or store-bought vegan blue cheese dressing (optional), for dipping

Preheat the oven to 450°F (230°C, or gas mark 8). Line a 9 x 13-inch (23 x 33-cm) baking sheet with parchment paper, leaving an overhang of 2 inches (5 cm) on one end of the baking sheet.

Stretch or roll out the pizza dough to fit the pan. Brush 1 tablespoon (15 ml) of the olive oil over the dough. Bake for 6 minutes, or until just starting to bubble. Remove from the oven and poke any bubbles with a fork.

Spread the sauce over the dough, and top with half of the mozzarella, the bell pepper, onion, mushrooms, sausage, and olives. Top with the remaining mozzarella and bake for 6 additional minutes, or until the crust has started to brown.

Remove from the oven. Use oven mitts or handle with caution in the following steps. Use the overhanging piece of parchment paper to lift the end of the pizza up and carefully start rolling it onto itself like a burrito. Roll the pizza all the way up until it looks like a large open-ended burrito. You can wait for the crust to cool a bit before you handle, but the longer you wait, the less pliable the crust will be, making it harder to roll up.

Brush the remaining 1 tablespoon (15 ml) olive oil all over the outside of the pizza burrito. Return to the oven and bake for 6 minutes, or until golden brown.

Cool for 10 minutes before cutting in half. Serve with blue cheese dressing (if using), for dipping.

Yield: 1 gigantic pizza burrito

Tip

Using your hands is very much in line with the theme of this book, so grab this beast with your hands, and sink your teeth in. Don't like the toppings on a supreme pizza? That's the coolest thing about this recipe! Do what you want; use your favorite pizza toppings to make a customized pizza burrito.

STUFFED-CRUST MEATBALL PARM PIZZA

The stuffed-crust pizza from a certain popular pizza chain was what dreams were made of for me as a kid! I thought it wouldn't be possible to enjoy that stuffed crust going vegan, but then vegan cheeses started improving so much that now it's one of my favorite nostalgic re-creations. Adding meatball parm to the stuffed crust ... that's just epic.

▼ 1 batch Pizza Dough (page 57), divided, enough for 1 pizza (see Tip on page 57)

▼ 1 block (8 ounces/227 g) vegan mozzarella, cut into eight sticks ½-inch (1-cm) in diameter

▼ 1 cup Beet Marinara (page 40), or store-bought marinara

▼ ½ cup (60 g) vegan mozzarella shreds

▼ ¼ cup Saucy Mozzarella (page 45, optional)

▼ 6 Meatballs (page 19) or store-bought vegan meatballs, cooked and halved (see Tip)

▼ 1 teaspoon Italian seasoning

▼ Quinoa Bacon Bits (page 14, optional)

▼ Crushed red pepper flakes (optional)

▼ Hemp Parmesan (page 14), or store-bought vegan parmesan (optional)

▼ 2 tablespoons (30 ml) olive oil, for drizzling

Preheat the oven to 450°F (230°C, or gas mark 8). Lightly dust a 12-inch (30-cm) pizza pan with all-purpose flour.

On a lightly floured surface, stretch or roll out the dough to 16 inches (39-cm) in diameter. Transfer to the prepared pizza pan, overlapping the pan by 2 inches (5 cm).

Place the mozzarella sticks on the dough sitting on the edge of the pan, 1 to 2 inches (2.5 to 5 cm) apart from each other, all the way around the perimeter. Fold the overhanging crust tightly over the mozzarella. Press the overlap into the dough to secure it over the mozzarella.

Top the center of the dough with the marinara sauce, mozzarella shreds, Saucy Mozzarella (if using), meatballs, and Italian seasoning. Sprinkle with desired amounts of bacon bits, crushed red pepper, and parmesan (if using). Drizzle 1 tablespoon (15 ml) of the olive oil on the edge of the crust and brush the crust evenly; drizzle the remaining 1 tablespoon (15 ml) olive oil over the pizza toppings.

Bake for 20 to 22 minutes, or until the edges and bottom of the crust have browned and the cheese has melted. Cool for 10 minutes, until easier to handle, and cut into 8 slices.

Yield: 4 to 8 servings

Tip

Meatballs should be prepared ahead of time to ensure thorough cooking. Once they've been cooked, let them cool for a few minutes before halving them. The addition of olive oil on the crust aids in giving it a nice golden crisp, while a drizzle of olive oil over the top adds some flavor. Bonus if you have infused olive oil on hand for drizzling! If you are watching your oil intake, feel free to omit completely.

UPSIDE-DOWN DEEP-DISH PIZZA

When I was a kid, I remember seeing a recipe in a magazine for an upside-down deep-dish pizza, and I always wanted to make it. As years passed, I forgot about it. During the process of writing this book, I was cleaning out my office one day when a magazine clipping with the original version of this pizza fell out of a pile of papers and literally into my lap. I took it as a sign and got to veganizing it ASAP—you just can't ignore signs like this from the universe, y'all! And I'm glad I didn't; I hope you love this pizza as much as I do.

- ▼ Cooking spray

- ▼ 3 tablespoons (45 ml) olive oil, divided, plus more as needed

- ▼ 1 bag (10 to 13 ounces, or 280 to 369 g) vegan beef crumbles

- ▼ 1 small onion, chopped

- ▼ 2 cups (142 g) broccoli florets (just the florets), cut into bite-size pieces

- ▼ 1 tablespoon (3 g) Italian seasoning

- ▼ 2½ cups Beet Marinara (page 40) or 1 jar (24 ounces or 613 g) store-bought marinara

- ▼ 1½ cups (175 g) vegan mozzarella shreds

- ▼ 1 batch Pizza Dough (page 57), divided, enough for 1 pizza (see Tip on page 57)

Preheat the oven to 425°F (220°C, or gas mark 7). Lightly coat a 9-inch (23-cm) pie pan with cooking spray.

Heat 2 tablespoons (30 ml) of the oil in a large skillet over medium heat. Add the beef crumbles and onion; sauté for 4 minutes, or until the onion is softened. Add the broccoli and Italian seasoning, stir to combine, and sauté an additional 4 minutes, or until the broccoli is fork-tender. Add the marinara, stir well, cover, reduce heat to low, and simmer for 5 minutes.

Transfer the mixture to the prepared pie pan, spreading it out evenly. Sprinkle the mozzarella over the top.

On a floured surface, stretch or roll out the dough to 10 to 12 inches (26 to 30 cm) in diameter. Set it over the top of the filling, and tuck the overhanging crust into the edge of the pan (between the filling and the pan). Drizzle the remaining 1 tablespoon (15 ml) olive oil over the dough and brush it to the edges, using more if needed. Pierce the center of the pie 4 times with a fork.

Bake for 20 to 22 minutes, or until the crust has puffed up and turned golden brown. Cool for 10 minutes before cutting into 8 slices.

Yield: 4 to 8 servings

Tip

Residual filling will inevitably fall off the pie slicer or spatula when transferring slices to serving plates. The good news is that this crust isn't delicate like pie crust; lift the crust up and return that filling to where it belongs to get that epic height out of each slice.

CHEESESTEAK PIZZA

Obviously the Philly cheesesteak sandwich is one of the best inventions, ever. And so is pizza, which is exactly why these two had to meet! The perfect crispy crust paired with hearty sandwich filling drizzled in luscious Cheesiest Cheese Sauce (page 44) is a combination that never gets old, no matter if it's in the form of a pizza or sandwich. This is also an awesome addition to a Sunday sports-watching spread!

- ▼ 1 batch Pizza Dough (page 57), divided, enough for 1 pizza (see Tip on page 57)

- ▼ Olive oil, for drizzling

- ▼ 1½ cups The Cheesiest Cheese Sauce (page 44)

- ▼ Philly Cheesesteaks filling (page 20)

- ▼ Hemp Parmesan (page 14) or store-bought vegan parmesan (optional)

- ▼ Scallions, roughly chopped (optional)

Preheat the oven to 450°F (230°C, or gas mark 8), and lightly dust a round 12-inch (30-cm) pizza pan with flour.

On a floured surface, roll out or stretch the dough to 12 inches (30 cm) and transfer to the prepared pizza pan. Drizzle olive oil over the crust, and then use a pastry brush to spread the oil over the entire crust. Bake for 6 minutes and then remove from the oven.

Spread ⅔ of the cheese sauce over the crust, top with cheesesteak filling and drizzle the remaining cheese sauce over the top. Place the pizza back in the oven and bake for an additional 12 minutes, until bubbly and the crust is browned on the edges and bottom.

Sprinkle with parmesan and scallions, if using. Cut into 8 slices and serve.

Yield: 8 slices

Tip

If you like heat, add a drizzle of Sriracha hot sauce when this pizza comes out of the oven—the combination of cheesy goodness and Sriracha is delicious! If by some chance you have used a spicy sausage in your cheesesteak mix, use Sriracha with caution.

CRAB RANGOON PIZZA

My husband, David, once came home from being on tour with work ranting and raving about this crab rangoon pizza he had at some pizza place that he couldn't remember the name of. Well, when David loves something, it becomes my mission to veganize it as fast as I can and get it to the table for dinner. I'm happy to say this didn't disappoint!

- ▼ 1 batch Pizza Dough (page 57), divided, enough for 1 pizza (see Tip on page 57)
- ▼ 1 tablespoon (15 ml) olive oil
- ▼ 2 batches Crab Rangoon filling (page 30)
- ▼ ¼ cup (30 g) vegan mozzarella shreds or Saucy Mozzarella (page 45)
- ▼ 2 tablespoons (30 ml) canola oil
- ▼ 2 vegan wonton wrappers, cut into strips
- ▼ ¼ cup Sweet Thai Chili Sauce (page 46), warmed
- ▼ 2 scallions, chopped or thinly sliced on the bias
- ▼ ½ teaspoon black sesame seeds

Preheat the oven to 450°F (230°C, or gas mark 8). Lightly dust a 12-inch (30-cm) pizza pan with all-purpose flour.

On a lightly floured surface, stretch or roll out the dough to 12 inches (30 cm). Transfer to the prepared pizza pan, and brush the olive oil over the entire dough. Bake for 6 minutes, and remove from the oven.

Spread the rangoon filling in an even layer over the crust and top with the mozzarella. Bake for an additional 12 minutes, or until the filling is bubbly and the crust is browned on the edges and bottom.

While the pizza is baking, line a small plate with paper towels.

Heat the canola oil in a small skillet over medium-high heat. Add the wonton strips and fry for 5 to 15 seconds, or until crisped and golden; transfer to the paper towel–lined plate. When cool to the touch, crush into smaller pieces.

Drizzle the finished pizza with the Thai chili sauce, then sprinkle with the crushed wontons, scallions, and sesame seeds. Cut into 8 slices, and serve hot.

Yield: 4 to 8 servings

Tip

Vegan wontons can be found at health food or international foods stores. I prefer the store-bought mozzarella for this pizza because it's already so sauce heavy, but the Saucy Mozzarella from the book ain't no slouch and does the job just as well.

UNICORN FRENCH BREAD PIZZA

Why do people obsess over unicorns? Because unicorns are magical. Why do people love pizza? Because pizza is also magical. So there, magic. What else? Unicorns are also beautiful and majestic, so put those gorgeous unicorn colors on a pizza and you have the perfect delight for any LGBTQ pride party because everyone—I repeat, EVERYONE—is beautiful and majestic and deserves to eat pizza that reflects just that. One might call this Pride Pizza.

▼ 1 long French baguette

▼ 2 cups Beet Marinara (page 40)

▼ 1 cup Saucy Mozzarella (page 45), or store-bought vegan mozzarella shreds

▼ Edible flowers, variety of colors

▼ Hemp Parmesan (page 14), nutritional yeast, or store-bought vegan parmesan

▼ Crushed red pepper flakes

▼ 8 small basil leaves

Preheat the oven to 425°F (220°C, or gas mark 7). Line a baking sheet with parchment paper.

Using a serrated knife, quarter the baguette crosswise to get 4 pieces, then cut each piece down the middle lengthwise to create the base for the French bread pizzas; you need 8 (6 to 8-inch [15 to 20-cm] long) pieces.

On each piece spread ¼ cup marinara, then drizzle or sprinkle with 2 tablespoons (33 g) mozzarella. Set on the prepared baking sheet. Bake for 10 to 12 minutes, or until the edges of the crust start to brown.

Remove from the oven and sprinkle with the edible flower petals, parmesan, and crushed red pepper. Place 1 beautiful basil leaf on each piece, and serve warm.

Yield: 8 servings

Tip

Most Whole Foods Markets carry edible flowers in the produce section where fresh herbs are found. But don't be shy; use that Internet and find edible flowers near you. Get the brightest variety of petals you can find to really achieve the unicorn flare. Or just go without and enjoy what will still be a colorful pizza, full of flavor!

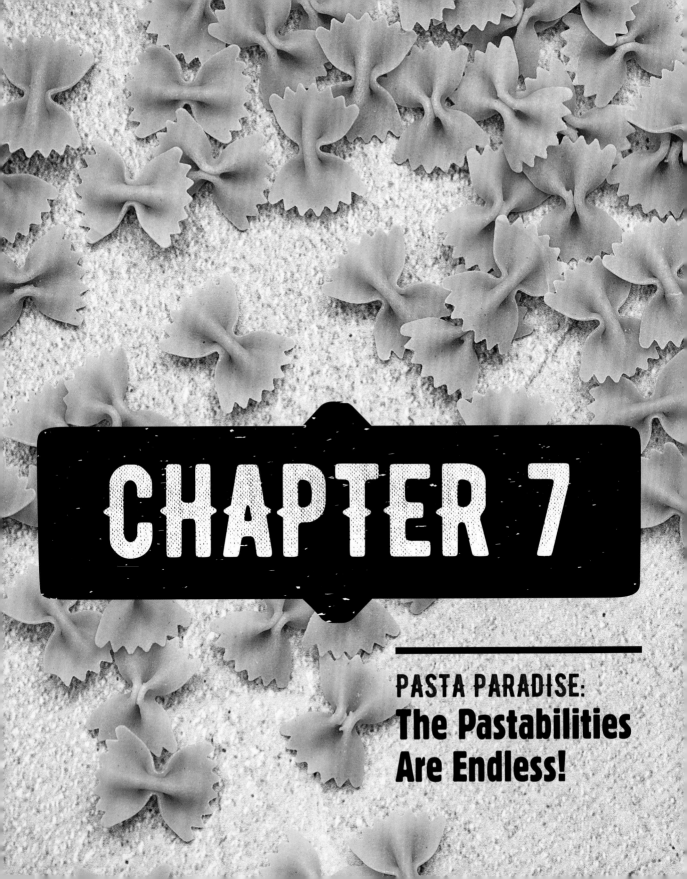

CHAPTER 7

PASTA PARADISE:
**The Pastabilities
Are Endless!**

SPINACH AND ARTICHOKE STUFFED SHELLS

Every epic recipe doesn't have to mean several recipes piled on top of each other—this recipe proves just that! Spinach and artichoke dip is delish, am I right? Who needs to dip pieces of toast into a communal dip bowl or appetizer when you can have a plate of jumbo stuffed shells all to yourself?

- ▼ 1 box (12 ounces or 340 g) jumbo pasta shells
- ▼ 1 tablespoon (15 ml) olive oil
- ▼ 1 onion, chopped
- ▼ 3 cloves garlic, minced
- ▼ 2 tablespoons (32 g) white miso
- ▼ 1 block (14 ounces or 397 g) extra-firm tofu, drained and pressed (see Tip, page 127)
- ▼ ½ cup (115 g) vegan mayonnaise
- ▼ 1 can (14 ounces or 397 g) quartered artichoke hearts, drained and roughly chopped
- ▼ 1 package (10 ounces or 280 g) frozen spinach, thawed and squeezed dry (see Tip)

- ▼ 1 cup (60 g) vegan mozzarella shreds
- ▼ Juice of 1 lemon
- ▼ 1½ teaspoons sea salt
- ▼ 1½ teaspoons black pepper
- ▼ 2½ cups Beet Marinara (page 40), or 1 jar (24 ounces) store-bought marinara
- ▼ Hemp Parmesan (page 14), or store-bought vegan parmesan
- ▼ Roughly chopped fresh basil

Prepare the pasta shells by cooking them according to package directions until just tender but still firm. Do not overcook; they will cook further in the oven. Drain the shells and set aside on a lightly oiled baking sheet to cool.

Heat the olive oil in a medium skillet over medium heat. Add the onion and sauté for 3 to 5 minutes, or until softened. Add the garlic and sauté 1 additional minute, until fragrant.

Transfer the onion-and-garlic mixture to a large bowl. Add the miso, and mix until the onions and garlic are coated. Crumble the tofu into the mixture. Add the mayonnaise, artichokes, spinach, mozzarella, lemon juice, salt, and pepper. Mix everything together until well combined.

Preheat the oven to 400°F (200°C, or gas mark 6). Stuff each shell with the spinach mixture, using your hands or a spoon to generously fill each shell.

Lightly coat a 9 x 13-inch (23 x 33-cm) baking dish with cooking spray and then spread half of the sauce accross the bottom of the dish. Arrange the shells, openings facing up; it will be a snug fit! Cover with the remaining sauce. Bake for 30 minutes, or until the cheesy tops begin to brown slightly.

Transfer to serving plates, and sprinkle with parmesan and basil.

Yield: 6 servings

Tip

It is imperative the spinach has been thoroughly squeezed dry to eliminate excess water. A quick way to achieve this is to wrap the spinach in paper towels and squeeze until the excess water is released. Repeat as needed until you have squeezed the last drop you possibly can from those greens!

CREAMY JAMBALAYA PASTA WITH CRISPY CHICKEN

Traditionally, the base of jambalaya includes sausage and another type of meat or seafood. For this version, I wanted to put the Fried Chicken (page 23) from the basics chapter to use. However, if you are short on time, by all means, pick up some vegan crispy chicken tenders at the store; it will be just as tasty. While jambalaya is usually on the spicier side, this recipe still packs a little punch but leans more on neutral for those who don't like spice; if you are the spicy type, see the Tip for how to heat things up!

For Sauce:

- 2 tablespoons (30 ml) olive oil
- 1 white onion, chopped
- 6 cloves garlic, roughly chopped
- 2 cups (457 ml) vegetable broth
- 1 cup (137 g) raw cashews, soaked in water overnight or boiled for 10 minutes and drained
- 2 tablespoons (6 g) Creole seasoning
- 2 teaspoons (10 ml) distilled white vinegar

For Pasta:

- 1 box (1 pound/454 g) farfalle (bow tie) pasta
- 2 tablespoons (30 ml) olive oil
- 2 cups (224 g) frozen cut okra
- 1 small red onion, chopped
- 1 red bell pepper, chopped
- 4 vegan sausages, sliced
- 1 can (14.5 ounces/411 g) diced tomatoes
- 12 pieces Fried Chicken (page 23), or store-bought crispy vegan chicken tenders, prepared and cut into ½-inch-thick (1-cm) strips
- Chopped fresh parsley
- Hemp Parmesan (page 14, optional)
- Crushed red pepper flakes (optional)

To make the sauce: Heat the oil in a large skillet over medium heat. Sauté the onion for 3 to 5 minutes, or until softened. Add the garlic and sauté 1 additional minute, until fragrant.

Transfer the onion mixture to a high-speed blender along with the broth, cashews, seasoning, and vinegar. Blend for 2 minutes, or until smooth and creamy.

To make the pasta: Prepare the pasta according to package directions; drain and set aside.

Heat the oil in the large saucepan or pot you cooked the pasta in over medium heat. Add the okra, onion, bell pepper, and sausages. Sauté for 8 minutes, stirring every 2 minutes, until the sausages have slightly browned and the vegetables have softened. Add the diced tomatoes with their juice, stir until well combined, and cook for 2 additional minutes, until heated through.

Add the prepared pasta and sauce, stirring until well combined. Divide among bowls. Top with the chicken strips and parsley. If desired, sprinkle with the parmesan and crushed red pepper.

Yield: 8 servings

Tip

While this recipe is on the spicy side, it can be spicier! If you like extra heat, add some crushed red pepper or cayenne pepper into the sauce mixture when blending until you reach the desired heat. Also sprinkle lots of crushed red pepper on top; I love my crushed red pepper!

FRENCH ONION PASTA BAKE WITH PIZZA CROUTONS

There is nothing more comforting and welcoming than a bowl of hot French onion soup with its savory broth and delicious crouton draped in melted Gruyère cheese. But I got to thinking: How nice would it be if I could bake up a big batch of something similar that I could bring to the table to serve a group of people all at once? Not only that, the flavors of French onion soup paired with pasta ... I couldn't resist. For an added flavor bonus, the crouton here isn't just a standard piece of bread but some bomb-ass pizza croutons instead; it's a flavor tornado up in these soup crocks! Can you handle this epicness?

For Pizza Croutons:

- ▼ 3 tablespoons (45 ml) olive oil
- ▼ 1 tablespoon (16 g) tomato paste
- ▼ 1 tablespoon (5 g) nutritional yeast
- ▼ 1 teaspoon Italian seasoning
- ▼ ¼ teaspoon sea salt
- ▼ ¼ teaspoon black pepper
- ▼ Vegan French baguette or Italian bread, cut or torn into 1½-inch (3.5-cm) cubes (about 2 cups)

For Pasta:

- ▼ ¼ cup (55 g) vegan butter
- ▼ 1 large onion, sliced
- ▼ 8 ounces (225 g) baby bella or white button mushrooms, stemmed and sliced
- ▼ 3 cloves garlic, minced
- ▼ 2 tablespoons (20 g) organic dark brown sugar
- ▼ ¾ cup (175 ml) red wine
- ▼ 2 tablespoons (28 ml) soy sauce
- ▼ 4 cups (940 ml) vegetable broth
- ▼ 1 cup (235 ml) water
- ▼ ½ teaspoon sea salt
- ▼ ¼ teaspoon black pepper
- ▼ 2 bay leaves
- ▼ 3 sprigs fresh thyme, plus more for garnish
- ▼ 1 box (1 pound/454 g) cavatappi pasta
- ▼ 2 batches Saucy Mozzarella (page 45), divided
- ▼ Hemp Parmesan (page 14) or store-bought vegan parmesan (optional)

To make the pizza croutons:

Preheat the oven to 375°F (190°C, or gas mark 5). Line a baking sheet with parchment paper.

In a medium bowl, whisk together the olive oil, tomato paste, nutritional yeast, Italian seasoning, salt, and pepper. Toss the cubed bread with the mixture until well coated. Transfer to the prepared baking sheet and bake for 4 minutes. Stir and bake for an additional 4 minutes, or until the croutons are starting to blacken slightly. Remove from the oven; set aside.

To make the pasta: Melt the

butter in a large saucepan or pot over medium-high heat. Add the onion and mushrooms; sauté for 5 minutes, or until soft. Add the garlic and brown sugar; sauté for 1 additional minute, until fragrant.

Add the wine and soy sauce. Turn the heat to high and cook for 12 to 14 minutes, or until the wine has cooked off completely.

Add the vegetable broth, water, salt, pepper, bay leaves, and thyme to the pot and bring to a boil. Add the pasta (the liquid will just barely cover). Cook, stirring frequently, according to the time indicated on the package directions (or longer if needed) until the pasta is al dente. The liquid will evaporate only a little during cooking. When the time is up, **do not drain the liquid.**

Add 1 cup (260 g) of the mozzarella, and stir it into the pasta until well combined. Cover, return the pot to high heat, and cook for 2 minutes. Remove from the heat and let sit for 5 minutes, still covered.

Preheat the oven to broil.

Remove the bay leaves and thyme from the pasta mixture; transfer the mixture to 4 individual 12-ounce (355 ml) soup crocks.

Place 3 or 4 croutons on top of the pasta in the center of each crock. Drizzle or spoon a heaping ¼ cup (65 g) of the mozzarella over the top of the croutons, covering the croutons to prevent them from burning. Broil for 2 to 4 minutes, or until the top of the cheese begins to brown slightly.

Remove from the broiler and sprinkle with parmesan, if using, and thyme leaves. Serve hot—be sure to caution your guests about the hot crocks!

Yield: 4 servings

Tip

The point of cooking the pasta in the broth and not draining it is to maintain the rich flavors French onion is known for as the starches from the pasta help create a creamy texture. If you don't have individual crocks, don't sweat it! Transfer the pasta mixture to a 9 x 13-inch (23 x 33-cm) baking dish, top with croutons and mozzarella, and bake as directed for the same tasty outcome.

ALMOST FAMOUS BUFFALO CHICKEN LASAGNA

I once made a 5-ingredient buffalo chicken dip for the 5-ingredient challenge segment of *The Vegan Roadie.* I have been looking for the opportunity to revisit that ever since. The minute I put a Blue Cheese Dressing recipe (page 42) in this book, I knew this was the right time! The combination of spicy and cool flavors between the sauce and dressing, paired with the savory chicken and pasta, can't be beat.

For Chicken:

- ▼ 2 tablespoons (30 ml) olive oil
- ▼ 2 cups cubed (1 inch/3 cm) Simply Seitan (page 22), or store-bought seitan or vegan chicken
- ▼ 1 onion, chopped
- ▼ 1 cup (110 g) shredded carrots
- ▼ ½ cup (50 g) chopped celery
- ▼ 4 cloves garlic, minced

For Blue Cheese Ricotta:

- ▼ 2 blocks (14 ounces/396 g) extra-firm tofu, drained and pressed (see Tip)
- ▼ 1 batch Blue Cheese Dressing (page 42)
- ▼ 2 tablespoons (30 g) tahini
- ▼ 2 tablespoons (30 g) Dijon mustard
- ▼ 1 teaspoon sea salt

For Buffalo Cream Sauce:

- ▼ 1 cup (137 g) raw cashews, soaked in water overnight or boiled for 10 minutes and drained
- ▼ 1½ cups (355 ml) water
- ▼ 1 batch Buffalo Sauce (page 84)

For Lasagna:

- ▼ Cooking spray
- ▼ 9 oven-ready lasagna noodles or traditional boiled lasagna noodles
- ▼ 2 cups (230 g) vegan mozzarella shreds
- ▼ 1 tablespoon (15 ml) olive oil
- ▼ Chopped fresh parsley
- ▼ Hemp Parmesan (page 14), or store-bought vegan parmesan (optional)

To make the chicken: Heat the oil in a large skillet over medium heat. Add the seitan, onion, carrots, and celery. Sauté for 6 minutes, stirring occasionally, until the seitan has started to brown. Add the garlic and sauté 1 to 2 minutes, until fragrant. Remove from the heat and set aside.

To make the blue cheese ricotta: Crumble the tofu into a medium bowl. Add the dressing, tahini, mustard, and salt. Stir everything together until well combined. Set aside.

To make the buffalo cream sauce: Add the cashews, water, and buffalo sauce to a high-speed blender. Blend for 2 minutes, or until creamy and smooth.

To assemble and bake the lasagna: Preheat the oven to 400°F (200°C, or gas mark 6). Lightly coat a 9 x 13-inch (23 x 33-cm) baking dish with cooking spray.

Spread ½ cup (120 ml) buffalo cream sauce on the bottom of the prepared dish. Arrange 3 lasagna noodles across the pan. Spread half of the blue cheese ricotta over the noodles and top that with half of the chicken mixture, followed by ½ cup (120 ml) buffalo cream sauce and ½ cup (about 65 g) mozzarella. Make sure the noodles are entirely covered. Repeat layering, starting with a layer of 3 noodles, then the remaining blue cheese ricotta, the remaining chicken mixture, ½ cup

(120 ml) buffalo cream sauce, and ½ cup (about 65 g) mozzarella. Top with one last layer of noodles and use the remaining buffalo cream sauce to cover the top, spreading the sauce so the noodles are completely covered. Sprinkle with the remaining 1 cup (about 130 g) mozzarella and drizzle the olive oil over the top.

Cover with aluminum foil and bake for 25 minutes. Remove the foil and bake an additional 10 minutes, or until the cheese has melted. Allow to cool for 15 minutes before cutting.

Garnish with parsley and parmesan, if desired.

Yield: 8 servings

Tip

To press the tofu, wrap the block tightly in dry paper towels. Place the wrapped tofu in a colander set in the kitchen sink. Set a small plate on top of the tofu and stack something heavy on top of it (like canned food). Let it sit for 20 minutes to release the water, unwrap, and it's ready for use. You can also use a tofu press for this. It's an inexpensive device and perfect for the environmentally conscious. I love the tofu press that I ordered online and use it often.

Almost Famous Buffalo Chicken Lasagna, page 126

LOBSTER MAC AND CHEESE

People go gaga over lobster mac and cheese. To be honest, I'm a sauce-and-pasta kind of guy; I've never enjoyed veggies or proteins mixed into my creamy pasta. Until this! I love the balance of flavors and the crunchy crust on top, and I hope you will too.

▼ Canola oil or cooking spray

▼ 1 batch Lobster Rolls filling (page 24)

▼ 1 batch Easy Creamy Shells and Cheese (page 16)

▼ ½ cup (56 g) crushed potato chips

▼ 2 tablespoons (10 g) nutritional yeast

▼ Smoked paprika (optional)

Preheat the oven to 400°F (200°C, or gas mark 6). Lightly coat a 9 x 13-inch (23 x 33-cm) baking dish with canola oil or cooking spray.

In a large bowl, mix together the Lobster Rolls filling and the Easy Creamy Shells and Cheese. Transfer to the prepared baking dish and bake for 15 minutes. Sprinkle with the potato chips and nutritional yeast. Bake an additional 15 to 20 minutes, or until the edges are crispy and browned.

Remove from the oven and cool for 10 minutes. Sprinkle the top with smoked paprika, if desired.

Yield: 8 servings

Tip

For an extra taste of the sea, don't be afraid to add an additional tablespoon or more of dulse flakes when you mix together the pasta and the lobster filling. The fishy taste in the Lobster Rolls filling is not as strong when added to the Easy Creamy Shells and Cheese, which creates a nice balance in flavors—but no judgment if you want to throw that balance a little out of whack and get your dulse on!

BAKED SPAGHETTI AND MEATBALL PIE

My mom used to make baked spaghetti when I was growing up; it was one of my favorite dishes, and I was trying to think of how I could expand on that favorite dish. I used the Meet the Meats Meatballs on page 18, mixed with cheese, marinara, and spaghetti to create those traditional flavors we all love housed in the biggest, most delicious slice of pie imaginable. I like to top it off with extra sauce and a nice big sprig of parsley, for that epic touch.

For the Pie Dough:

- 2½ cups (314 g) all-purpose flour
- 1 tablespoon (3 g) Italian seasoning
- 1 teaspoon sea salt
- 1 cup (225 g) cold vegan butter, cut into small pieces
- ½ cup (120 ml) ice water, plus more if needed

For the Pie:

- 1 box (1 pound/454 g) spaghetti
- Canola oil or cooking spray
- 2½ cups Beet Marinara (page 40), or 1 jar (24 ounces or 613 g) store-bought marinara, plus more for serving (optional)
- 3 cups (about 12) Meatballs (page 18), or store-bought meatballs, cooked and quartered
- 1½ cups (175 g) vegan mozzarella shreds
- Parsley sprigs (optional)

To make the dough: In a large bowl, whisk together the flour, Italian seasoning, and salt. Cut the butter into the mixture with a fork, pastry cutter, or your fingers until it develops a crumbly, sand-like consistency. Using a spatula, mix in the ice water, starting with ¼ cup (60 ml), then adding 1 tablespoon (15 ml) at a time as needed. Mix until the dough just comes together, using more water if needed. Do not overmix. Cut the dough in half and shape into 2 flat discs, wrap in plastic wrap and place in the refrigerator while cooking pasta.

To make the pie: Prepare the pasta according to package directions; drain and set aside.

Preheat the oven to 375°F (190°C, or gas mark 5). Lightly coat a 9-inch (23-cm) pie pan with canola oil or cooking spray.

On a lightly floured surface, roll one disc of the dough to an 11-inch (28-cm) circle, ¼ inch (6 mm) thick. Transfer the dough to the prepared pie pan; the sides of the dough will fall over the edge. Roll the other disc of the dough to a 10-inch (25-cm) circle; set aside.

In a large bowl, mix together the prepared spaghetti, marinara, meatballs, and mozzarella until well combined and the meatball quarters are evenly dispersed. Transfer the mixture to the dough in the pie pan and lay the second piece of the pie dough over the filling.

Fold the edges of the bottom dough into the top one and crimp the dough between your fingertips to make a decorative border. With a sharp knife, cut 4 small slits in the center of the top layer of dough.

Bake for 50 to 55 minutes, or until the crust is golden brown. Cool the pie for at least 10 minutes before cutting into 8 slices.

Top each slice with more marinara and parsley to garnish, if desired.

Yield: 8 servings

Tip

Make the meatballs, pie dough, and marinara the day before, and the next day is easy-peasy assembly! If the dough is too hard to roll out when it comes out of the refrigerator, let it set at room temperature for a few minutes until it becomes more malleable. This pie will last up to 4 days in the refrigerator to enjoy as leftovers; it happens to be one of those recipes that is super delicious in leftover form.

DAVID'S CARBY CARBONARA

If there is one thing we love in my home, it's carbs! We make an effort to remain as balanced as we can but sometimes a big bowl of pasta is just too hard to resist! When I filmed *The Vegan Roadie Season 3: Ciao Italia*, I was overjoyed at the numerous plates of vegan carbonara I was served while in Italy. Carbonara in itself is just epic with its creamy sauce and smoky flavors. I was so inspired that I created this one for a pop-up dinner at a fantastic restaurant in Brooklyn called Adelina's. My husband, David, helped me test this recipe over and over to get that buttery decadent balance just right! We hope it becomes a staple at your family dinners as it has ours. They don't call him Mr. Rossetti for nothin'!

For Spaghetti:

- ▼ 1 box (1 pound/454 g) spaghetti (reserve ½ cup [120 ml] cooking water)
- ▼ Freshly ground black pepper (optional)
- ▼ Chopped parsley (optional)

For Sauce:

- ▼ 1 cup (240 g) silken or soft tofu
- ▼ ¼ cup (59 ml) olive oil
- ▼ ¼ cup (60 ml) reserved cooking water
- ▼ ¼ teaspoon minced garlic
- ▼ 1 teaspoon lemon juice
- ▼ 1¼ teaspoons smoked paprika
- ▼ ½ teaspoon sea salt
- ▼ ¼ teaspoon black pepper
- ▼ ½ teaspoon Himalayan black salt (kala namak, optional)
- ▼ 1 batch Quinoa Bacon Bits (page 14)

To make the spaghetti:
Prepare the pasta according to package directions. Reserve ½ cup (120 ml) cooking water and then drain; transfer to a large bowl.

To make the sauce:
Combine the tofu, olive oil, reserved cooking water, garlic, lemon juice, smoked paprika, salt, pepper, and black salt (if using) in a high-speed blender. Blend 1 minute, or until smooth and creamy.

Add the bacon bits and sauce to the bowl with the pasta. Mix with tongs until well combined. If the pasta is too dry add 1 tablespoon (14 ml) of water as needed to get the sauce and bacon bits incorporated until all of the pasta is coated and creamy.

Divide into 6 servings. Garnish with freshly cracked black pepper and parsley, if using.

Yield: 6 servings

Tip

A fun and traditional way to plate pasta is the "spool technique" and it's pretty easy to master! You do need to have a very large fork, dare I say a "meat fork" for the most efficient results. Spool a portion from the pot onto the fork and then slide a large spoon underneath the portion, transfer to a plate, slowly remove the spoon from underneath the spool of pasta and then gently push the pasta off the fork with the large spoon while pulling the fork out. Garnish and serve for an impressive look with your little mountain of pasta spooled high!

Pictured:
Baked Spaghetti and Meatball Pie, Red Wine Tempeh with Creamy Bucatini, David's Carby Carbonara, Chocolate Chickpea Ravioli

RED WINE TEMPEH WITH CREAMY BUCATINI

I created this tempeh marinade as one of my final exams when I was in culinary school. The instructor grading that day, Chef Hideyo, held on to my dish to have as her lunch. SCORE! I impressed one of my favorite chefs, who tasted several plates that day—I was on top of the world. I paired the tempeh with this pasta for a fun, vibrant, and colorful plate full of flavor, but I feel it would go just as nicely on a fresh green salad. I hope you like it!

For Bucatini:

- 1 box (1 pound/454 g) bucatini
- Hemp Parmesan (page 14), or store-bought vegan parmesan (optional)

For Tempeh:

- ⅔ cup (160 ml) red wine
- ½ cup (118 ml) olive oil
- 2 tablespoons (28 ml) soy sauce or tamari
- Juice of 1 lemon
- 3 cloves garlic, minced
- 1½ teaspoons dried thyme
- 1 teaspoon sea salt
- 1 teaspoon black pepper
- 1 block (8 ounces or 225 g) tempeh, cut into 16 slices

For Sauce:

- 2 tablespoons (30 ml) olive oil
- 1 onion, chopped
- ½ cup (112 g) peeled and chopped beets
- 6 cloves garlic, sliced
- 1 cup (137 g) raw cashews, soaked in water overnight or boiled for 10 minutes and drained
- 1 cup (235 ml) water
- ½ cup (120 ml) red wine
- 1 tablespoon (16 g) white miso
- 1 teaspoon sea salt

To make the bucatini:
Prepare the pasta according to package directions. Drain and transfer to a large bowl.

To make the tempeh: In a
high-speed blender, combine the wine, olive oil, soy sauce, lemon juice, garlic, thyme, salt, and pepper. Blend until smooth and emulsified, 1 to 2 minutes. Transfer the marinade to a medium skillet. Add the tempeh, bring to a boil, and reduce to a simmer. Cook for 10 minutes, flip, and cook for an additional 10 minutes. The liquid will evaporate slightly and the tempeh will darken in color to a beautiful burgundy hue.

Heat a separate skillet over medium heat. In 2 batches, transfer just the pieces of tempeh to the new skillet, and sear each side for 2 minutes. It will not be necessary to add more oil to the new skillet as the oil from the pieces of tempeh will cook off and coat the skillet. Set the tempeh aside on a plate, and use this skillet to make the sauce.

To make the sauce: Heat the
oil in the skillet over medium heat. Add the onion, beets, and garlic; sauté for 3 minutes, or until soft and fragrant. Transfer to a high-speed blender. Add the cashews, water, wine, miso, and salt. Blend about 2 minutes until smooth and creamy.

Transfer the sauce to the prepared pasta and toss with tongs until all the pasta is coated. Serve in large pasta bowls with 4 pieces of tempeh per serving, sprinkled with parmesan, if desired.

Yield: 4 servings

Tip

Don't like bucatini or can't find it? Just use the thickest long-strand noodles you can find, or use any pasta you like! I chose bucatini because I've always enjoyed the texture and because it has a hole through the center, like a straw! Cooking isn't that serious; have fun and choose things you like.

CHOCOLATE CHICKPEA RAVIOLI

One of my favorite parts of filming *The Vegan Roadie Season 3: Ciao Italia!* was getting hands-on in the kitchen of Italian families, making pasta from scratch, piling platters high with tomatoes and basil grown from their gardens, and drizzling freshly made olive oil on, well, everything. This recipe was inspired by the Naples episode in which I made a chestnut flour, for a *castagnaccio* filling, and housed it in fresh-made pasta for decadent chocolate ravioli. I replaced the chestnuts with chickpeas here for a quick fix with things that might already be in your pantry.

For Chickpea Filling:

▼ 1 can (15 ounces/426 g) chickpeas, drained and rinsed

▼ ¼ cup (22 g) unsweetened cocoa powder

▼ ¼ cup (30 g) organic confectioners' sugar

▼ 3 tablespoons (45 ml) agave

▼ ½ teaspoon sea salt

For Pasta:

▼ 2 cups (250 g) all-purpose flour

▼ ½ cup (120 g) silken tofu

▼ 2 tablespoons (40 g) maple syrup

▼ 2 tablespoons (30 ml) white wine or water

▼ 1 teaspoon sea salt

▼ Canola oil

▼ Organic confectioners' sugar

▼ Crackle and Fudgy Chocolate Sauce, fudgy option (page 51, optional)

To make the chickpea filling:
In a food processor, combine the chickpeas, cocoa powder, confectioners' sugar, agave, and salt. Process until well combined. Some texture will remain—it will not be completely smooth. Transfer to a bowl and refrigerate, uncovered, for 30 minutes, or until slightly chilled and thicker in consistency.

To make the pasta: In a cleaned food processor, combine the flour, tofu, maple syrup, wine, and salt. Process until an elastic ball of dough forms.

To make the ravioli: On a floured surface, roll out the dough to a 16 x 12-inch (40 x 30-cm) rectangle, with the long edge toward you. Cut a line down the center the long way, leaving you with two pieces of dough that are 16 x 6 inches (40 x 15 cm).

Prepare a small bowl of warm water for sealing the sides of the dough together.

On the bottom half of each strip of dough, place 6 dollops of the chickpea filling in a row, using 1 heaping tablespoon (14 g) for each dollop. Leave 1 inch (2.5 cm) between each dollop and 1 inch (2.5 cm) of space on the ends of each strip of dough.

Using your finger or a pastry brush, wet all the edges of the dough within 1 inch (2.5 cm) around each dollop of filling. Fold the top half of the dough over the filling and press down around the filling to seal the dough, working gently to remove any air bubbles from inside the ravioli. Use a knife, pastry cutter, or ravioli cutter to create 2-inch (5-cm) squares of ravioli. Repeat with the second strip of dough and the remaining filling.

In a large skillet, pour 1 inch (2.5 cm) of canola oil. Heat the oil to 350°F (175°C) when tested with a candy thermometer or until a tiny piece of dough placed in the oil fries up quickly and rises to the top. Line a plate with paper towels.

In 3 to 4 batches, using tongs, place the ravioli in the oil and fry for 20 to 30 seconds; flip and fry for 20 to 30 more seconds, until each side is golden brown. Transfer to the paper towel–lined plate.

Plate the ravioli on 1 platter and dust with confectioners' sugar. Alternatively, plate individual servings by drizzling the chocolate sauce over a plate, topping with 3 ravioli, and dusting with confectioners' sugar.

Yield: 4 servings (12 ravioli)

Tip

There will be scraps of dough left over from this and not enough filling to fill said scraps, as the amount of scraps will vary each time with the chef! But never fear; twist those scraps up, fry them quickly, and serve them on the plate with the ravioli, dusted with confectioners' sugar. I promise you, the scraps will disappear just as fast as the ravioli.

CHAPTER 8

BOWLS OF STUFF:
Fork It, Spoon It, Slurp It!

FRIED CHICKEN NOODLE SOUP

We all know chicken noodle soup has been touted as a household remedy to relieve common cold symptoms. And we all know fried chicken has been celebrated for making everyone happy at dinner, especially the fried chicken in this book because there ain't no chicken in it—hooray! Now imagine the miraculous wonders that must occur when you pair a magical soup with crispy, juicy, crowd-pleasing pieces of chicken! That's right: Unicorns take flight, world peace is among us, and your cold disappears. Okay, those results aren't guaranteed, but I *can* guarantee you will want a second helping! Keep your chicken crispy by adding it to the top just before serving.

- 2 tablespoons (30 ml) olive oil
- 2 carrots, thinly sliced
- 2 ribs celery, thinly sliced
- 1 onion, chopped
- 4 cloves garlic, minced
- 2 tablespoons (8 g) chopped fresh parsley, plus more for garnish
- 1 teaspoon sea salt
- ½ teaspoon black pepper
- 8 cups (1.9 l) vegetable or vegan chicken broth
- 1 box (1 pound/454 g) rotini pasta
- 1 batch Fried Chicken (page 23), cut into 1- to 2-inch (2.5 to 5-cm) pieces

Heat the oil in a stockpot over medium heat. Add the carrots, celery, and onion. Sauté for 5 to 7 minutes, or until the carrots are fork-tender. Add the garlic and sauté 1 additional minute, until fragrant.

Add the parsley, salt, and pepper. Mix well. Slowly add in the broth, cover, and bring to a boil. Add the pasta and cook, uncovered, until the pasta is al dente according to package directions.

Divide the soup among serving bowls and top each with ½ cup (142 g) of the Fried Chicken piled in the center. Garnish with more chopped parsley.

Yield: 6 to 8 servings

Tip

The rotini spirals are perfect for this soup. When they're done boiling, they continue to cook as they sit in the hot liquid; eventually they are large and soft, just like the egg noodles traditionally used in chicken noodle soup. The soup also gets thicker as it sits because of the starch from the pasta; add more broth, if needed, especially when eating leftovers. If using leftover chicken, reheat it in the oven at 350°F (175°C, or gas mark 4) on a baking sheet for 8 to 12 minutes until hot and crispy.

SAVORY CHEDDAR FONDUE WAFFLE BOWL

Oh. This. Waffle. I first had a version of this while filming an episode of *The Vegan Roadie* in Denver at a restaurant called City O' City. I have since taken it into my own hands, creating my own luscious fondue that is super decadent and smooth. Paired here with Sweet Potato Waffles and a fluffy scramble, it has won over the hearts of many vegans and nonvegans alike. I actually use it when I teach cooking classes, and it is always the class favorite, hands down.

- ▶ 2 tablespoons (30 ml) olive oil
- ▶ ½ head cauliflower, cut into small florets
- ▶ 1 cup (98 g) snow peas, trimmed and halved
- ▶ 2 medium carrots, thinly sliced on the bias
- ▶ 1 batch Eggsellent Eggs, scrambled (page 32)
- ▶ 4 Sweet Potato Waffles (page 70), quartered
- ▶ 1 batch Coconut-Cheddar Fondue (page 43), warmed
- ▶ Chopped chives (optional)

Heat the oil in a large skillet over medium heat. Add the cauliflower, peas, and carrots. Sauté 6 to 8 minutes, until the cauliflower and carrots are fork-tender but still crunchy. Mix in the scramble until well combined and heated through.

To serve, stack the quartered pieces of 1 waffle on top of each other in the center of a bowl. Top the waffle stack with ¼ of the scramble mixture and drizzle ¼ of the fondue sauce over it; the fondue will trickle to the bottom of the bowl and to the waffle. Sprinkle with chopped chives, if using.

Divide the remaining ingredients evenly among 3 more bowls.

Yield: 4 servings

Tip

Make this a chicken 'n waffles bowl by adding the Fried Chicken on page 23 and drizzling some Sriracha hot sauce over the final bowl for some heat! Also, I love this fondue so much I often double the recipe to be sure there is extra for those who like to get saucy!

LOADED BAKED POTATO SOUP WITH PRETZEL BOWLS

My first restaurant job was at Bennigan's. I worked with a lively bunch, some of whom I'm still friends with to this day. There were many hungover mornings of opening the restaurant that consisted of one hangover cure: the loaded baked potato soup. I've missed this soup, so I'm thrilled to bring it back, vegan style, and share it with you. Go the extra mile and serve it in a pretzel bowl for epic realness, or just enjoy as is!

▼ 3 pounds (1.4 kg) russet potatoes, scrubbed and cut in half

▼ 1 cup (137 g) raw cashews, soaked in water overnight or boiled for 10 minutes and drained

▼ 1 cup (235 ml) water

▼ ¼ cup (55 g) vegan butter

▼ 1 cup (160 g) chopped onion

▼ 4 cloves garlic, minced

▼ 4 cups (940 ml) vegetable broth

▼ 2 teaspoons (10 g) sea salt

▼ 1 teaspoon black pepper

▼ 1 cup (115 g) vegan cheddar shreds, plus more for garnish

▼ 4 scallions, chopped, divided

▼ 2 tablespoons Quinoa Bacon Bits (page 14), plus more for garnish

▼ 4 Pretzel Bowls (page 60)

Preheat the oven to 400°F (200°C, or gas mark 6). Line a baking sheet with parchment paper.

Place the potatoes, cut-side down, on the prepared baking sheet and bake for 35 to 40 minutes, or until tender when pierced with a fork. Remove from the oven and cool 15 minutes, or until cool enough to handle.

Meanwhile, in a high-speed blender, combine the cashews and water. Blend until smooth and creamy, 1 to 2 minutes.

Scoop out the insides of one-third of the potatoes; transfer to a bowl and mash. Scoop out the remaining potatoes and cut the flesh into ½-inch (1-cm) cubes; set aside in a separate bowl.

In a stockpot, melt the butter over medium heat. Add the onions and sauté for 3 to 5 minutes, or until softened. Add the garlic and sauté 1 additional minute, until fragrant.

Add the mashed potatoes, broth, salt, pepper, and blended cashew milk to the pot, and bring just to a simmer. Stir in the cubed potatoes and remove from the heat. Stir in the cheddar, 2 tablespoons (12 g) of the scallions, and bacon bits. Add more salt and pepper, to taste, if desired.

Divide the soup among the pretzel bowls, and garnish with more cheddar, the remaining scallions, and more bacon bits.

Yield: 4 servings in the bowls or 8 servings in regular bowls

Tip

Skip the Quinoa Bacon Bits if you are short on time, but don't skip the bacon altogether; use store-bought vegan bacon, chopped up into bits and sautéed until crispy.

KEEPIN' IT CLEAN BOWL

Obviously, this book's main purpose is to show that vegans eat more than salad; yet, we also love our salads—and there's no reason salads can't be epic! I included this epic salad bowl for those days when you are keeping it clean and green. Don't let the head-of-lettuce bowl intimidate you. Feel free to just make this in a regular bowl; you'll need to have only 1 head of lettuce for the entire recipe then. But I will say, the lettuce-head bowl is super fun for a lunch with friends!

For Dressing:

- ¼ cup (60 g) tahini
- Juice of 1 lemon
- 1 tablespoon (15 ml) maple syrup
- ¼ teaspoon sea salt
- 2 to 4 tablespoons (28 to 60 ml) water, as needed

For Salad:

- 4 large heads iceberg lettuce
- 1 cup (55 g) baby spinach
- 1 cup (71 g) broccoli florets, steamed
- ½ cup (75 g) frozen sweet peas, thawed
- ½ cup (90 g) frozen shelled edamame, thawed
- ½ cup (17 g) sprouts, pea shoots, or micro greens
- 1 can (15 ounces/426 g) chickpeas, drained and rinsed (roasted optional, see Tip)
- 1 avocado, peeled and sliced (see Tip, page 88)

For Garnish:

- 4 teaspoons (3 g) pepitas
- 2 teaspoons (5 g) hemp seeds
- Quinoa Bacon Bits (page 14, optional)

To make the dressing:

In a bowl, whisk together the tahini, lemon juice, maple syrup, and salt until smooth and creamy. Add water, if necessary, as tahini can differ in consistency; the water is helpful to achieve desired creaminess.

To make the lettuce bowl:

Cut the bottom off each head of lettuce, just enough to flatten it so it can sit sturdy in a large bowl or on a plate. Usually, cutting off anything from the size of a quarter to the size of the bottom of a drinking glass works.

Set the head of lettuce flat and take a sharp knife around the perimeter, cutting halfway down into and all the way around the head of lettuce. Remove anything that will come out on its own at this point; with the remainder, take a large metal spoon or ice cream scoop and gently scoop out the insides. Place the scooped-out lettuce from 1 head on a cutting board; reserve the rest from the other heads to make salads within the next few days.

To make the salad:
Put the spinach on a cutting board with the reserved lettuce from 1 head. Chop them together into smaller pieces.

Plate each lettuce bowl and divide the lettuce-spinach mixture among them. Top each with ¼ cup (18 g) broccoli florets, 2 tablespoons (18 g) peas, 2 tablespoons (22 g) edamame, 2 tablespoons (4 g) sprouts, ¼ of the chickpeas, and ¼ of the avocado. Keep the ingredients divided in their own sections; it creates a cleaner and more bountiful looking presentation.

Drizzle the dressing over each salad bowl and top each with 1 teaspoon pepitas, ½ teaspoon hemp seeds, and bacon bits (if desired).

Yield: 4 servings

Tip

If you have time and want a little crunch with your chickpeas, toss them with 1 tablespoon (15 ml) coconut oil and some salt and pepper. Transfer to a parchment-lined baking sheet and roast at 425°F (220°C, or gas mark 7) for 30 to 35 minutes, tossing around halfway through, until crispy.

WONTON BOWLS WITH GARLIC-FRIED QUINOA

Nothing is more fun than serving something up in dinnerware that is edible! These wonton bowls are super easy to make and fun to fill with fried quinoa or anything else you want! Feeling extra epic? Make the Crab Rangoon on page 30 and serve each bowl of garlic-fried quinoa topped off with a rangoon and a drizzle of Sweet Thai Chili Sauce (page 46)! Or be as basic as you dare and just make the super tasty Garlic-Fried Quinoa on its own (no judgment from me!). Who you trying to impress anyway!?

For Wonton Bowls:

- Cooking spray
- 24 wonton wrappers or 6 vegan egg roll wrappers

For Garlic Sauce:

- 2 teaspoons olive oil
- ½ cup (80 g) chopped onion
- 4 cloves garlic, chopped
- 1 teaspoon roughly chopped ginger
- 1 cup (235 ml) vegetable broth
- 1 tablespoon (15 ml) soy sauce
- 1 tablespoon (8 g) cornstarch
- 1 teaspoon rice vinegar
- ½ teaspoon sea salt
- ¼ teaspoon black pepper

For Garlic-Fried Quinoa:

- 1 tablespoon (15 ml) toasted sesame or olive oil
- 1 onion, chopped
- 2 cups (142 g) broccoli florets (just the florets), cut into bite-size pieces
- 1½ cups (225 g) frozen peas
- 3 cloves garlic, minced
- 1½ cups (about 165 g) julienned or grated carrots
- 1½ cups (105 g) shredded red cabbage
- 2 cups (370 g) cooked quinoa
- Sriracha hot sauce (optional)
- 3 scallions, chopped on a bias

To make the wonton bowls:

Preheat the oven to 350°F (175°C, or gas mark 4). Lightly coat a jumbo muffin tin with 6 cavities with cooking spray.

If using wonton wrappers, overlap 4 wrappers to create 1 large wrapper that is 6 x 6 inches (15 x 15 cm). Overlap the small wontons in the middle, wet the edges where they overlap, and press down to seal the pieces together to create the large wrapper. Repeat with the remaining wrappers until there are 6 larger ones.

Transfer the large wontons or egg roll wrappers to the prepared muffin tin and gently press each one into a cavity to create a bowl shape. Coat the wontons lightly with cooking spray.

Bake for 8 to 10 minutes, or until golden brown.

To make the sauce: Heat the oil in a large skillet over medium heat. Add the onions, garlic, and ginger; sauté for 3 to 5 minutes, or until the onions are softened and the mixture is fragrant.

Transfer the onion mixture to a high-speed blender. Add the broth, soy sauce, cornstarch, vinegar, salt, and pepper. Blend for 1 to 2 minutes, until smooth and creamy. Transfer back to the skillet set over medium-low heat. Cook about 3 minutes, or until it begins to bubble and thickens slightly. Transfer to a bowl.

To make the garlic-fried quinoa: Wipe out the skillet used for the sauce, add the oil, and set over medium-high heat. Add the onion, broccoli, and peas. Sauté 2 to 4 minutes, or until the broccoli is fork-tender.

Reduce the heat to medium and add the carrots and cabbage, mixing until well combined. Cook for 2 to 4 minutes, or until heated through. Add the quinoa and cook for an additional 2 minutes to heat through. Add the garlic sauce and mix well.

Divide the quinoa mixture among the wonton bowls. Drizzle with Sriracha, if using. Sprinkle with the scallions, and serve with a set of chopsticks sticking up out of the bowl.

Yield: 6 servings

Tip

This is an awesome go-to lunch item during the week. Prepare just the sauce and Garlic-Fried Quinoa, and you can even add the Eggsellent Eggs on page 32, baked and chopped up for some more protein. Portion into 2 to 4 containers for a quick on-the-go option during a busy week; leave the wonton bowls for another time!

BLESS-YOUR-HEART BOWL

This is the bowl you dive into when you want to have the arms of comfort wrapped around you. My father is from Alabama, and not an afternoon goes by when I visit that I don't hear a family member say, "Well, bless their heart..." which, for those of you not familiar, is a phrase that has multiple meanings. It can be sincere and sympathetic or also hold the weight of being a passive-aggressive way to insult someone. That being said, I gave this bowl that name because it certainly includes the comfort foods I would want to enjoy while in the South, should someone dare say "Bless your heart" to my face with the intention of either meaning!

- 1 teaspoon olive oil

- ½ onion, roughly chopped

- ½ cup (120 ml) vegetable broth

- 1 bunch collard greens, stemmed and roughly chopped

- ¼ teaspoon smoked salt or sea salt

- Pinch black pepper

- 4 cups Mom's Chili (page 25), or store-bought vegan chili

- 4 cups Easy Creamy Shells and Cheese (page 16), or store-bought boxed vegan macaroni and cheese, warmed

- 4 pieces Cornbread (see Tip, page 62)

Heat the oil in a large skillet over medium heat. Add the onion and sauté for 3 to 5 minutes, or until softened. Slowly add the vegetable broth and bring just to a simmer. Add the collards, salt, and pepper. Mix well with tongs. Cover and cook for 2 to 4 minutes, or until the collards have wilted. Uncover and cook an additional 1 to 2 minutes, tossing occasionally, until the liquid has evaporated. Add more salt and pepper to taste, if desired.

Add 1 cup chili and 1 cup cheesy shells to each of 4 bowls. Divide the collard greens among the bowls, and add a piece of cornbread to each.

Yield: 4 servings

Tip

The recipes in this bowl are all great things to make separately during the week for dinner. I like to make this bowl on a lazy Sunday when I have some leftovers from these individual recipes; just warm the mac and chili on the stovetop as you cook up the greens. Cornbread can be served at room temperature.

CHEESESTEAK BAKED POTATO BOWL

You can't get around it. There's a reason people love the cheesesteak combination of a hearty meat with peppers and onions slathered in cheese sauce: It's fudging scrumptious! And this bowl takes it a step further by adding some greens to the game (I will sneak those in any time I can!) and making a dull baked potato delicious. If you're not feeling the green, skip the kale and just make an epic cheesesteak baked potato.

- 4 russet potatoes, scrubbed and halved
- 1 tablespoon (15 ml) olive oil, plus more for potatoes
- 1 bunch kale, stemmed and chopped
- Sea salt
- Black pepper
- 1 batch Philly Cheesesteaks filling (page 20)
- 2 cups The Cheesiest Cheese Sauce (page 44)
- 2 scallions, chopped (optional)

Preheat the oven to 400°F (200°C, or gas mark 6). Line a baking sheet with parchment paper.

Using your hands, rub each potato half with a small amount of olive oil, until coated. Place the potatoes, cut-side down, on the prepared baking sheet and bake for 35 to 40 minutes, or until tender when pierced with a fork.

Heat the olive oil in a large skillet over medium heat. Add the kale and sauté, tossing with tongs, about 1 to 2 minutes, or until wilted. Season with salt and pepper to taste.

Divide the kale among 4 bowls. Place 2 potato halves in each bowl, cut-sides up. Smother each potato half with cheesesteak filling, then drizzle each bowl with ¼ to ½ cup of the cheese sauce. Sprinkle with chopped scallions, if desired.

Yield: 4 servings

Tip

This is a great way to utilize leftovers from the Philly Cheesesteaks on page 20; just warm them up on the stovetop when ready to use! If you don't have leftovers, though, you can easily make the filling (and the cheese sauce!) while the potatoes bake.

GRILLED ROMAINE BOWL WITH WHITE BBQ SAUCE

I've been waiting to share this delicious salad with the world, and I'm thrilled to bring its epicness to these pages! The crispy, charred romaine paired with the sweet and crunchy pepper and corn, doused in the tangy BBQ sauce, has won over many dinner guests at events that I have been the chef for in New York City. The white BBQ sauce is a product of the South and always fascinates northerners; paired with the smoky Quinoa Bacon Bits, it is a dish that surprises and delights every time! Serve as a main dish or an appetizer (see Tip). If you have access to a grill, skip the step of searing the romaine halves in a pan and grill those suckers until they have those beautiful charred grill marks.

- ▼ 4 teaspoons (20 ml) olive oil, divided
- ▼ 3 romaine hearts, halved, cut to size (see Tip)
- ▼ ½ cup White BBQ Sauce (page 48)
- ▼ 1 cup (164 g) corn, frozen or fresh
- ▼ ½ red bell pepper, uniformly diced small
- ▼ 3 tablespoons Quinoa Bacon Bits (page 14)
- ▼ 21 Cornbread Croutons (page 62)
- ▼ 2 scallions, chopped

Heat 1 teaspoon of the olive oil in a large skillet over medium heat. Add 2 romaine heart halves, cut-side down, and sear 2 to 4 minutes, or until the cut sides start to char; remove from the skillet and set aside. Repeat with 1 teaspoon of oil and 2 romaine halves at a time.

Add the last teaspoon of olive oil to the skillet. Sauté the corn for 6 to 8 minutes, tossing occasionally until lightly charred.

Build each bowl by placing 2 romaine halves, cut-sides up, crisscrossing over each other in a bowl. Drizzle with 2 heaping tablespoons (32 g) BBQ sauce and sprinkle with ¼ cup (41g) corn, ⅓ of the bell pepper, and 1 tablespoon (10 g) bacon bits. Place 7 croutons in the bowl, and garnish with a sprinkle of scallions.

Repeat with the remaining ingredients.

Yield: 3 main-dish salads or 6 appetizer salads

Tip

The romaine hearts should fit in a large shallow bowl crisscrossed over each other. Before grilling, size them to the bowl by cutting off any overflow from the top, maintaining the pointy shape of a romaine heart (rather than just lopping off the top). While this serves 3, it could easily serve 6 as an appetizer with 1 romaine half served on a single long plate; just divide the remaining ingredients 6 ways.

SHAKE IT OFF!:
Chill Sips for
Every Occasion

CHAPTER 9

ULTIMATE CARAMEL COOKIE BROWNIE SHAKE

I saw a shake once with a stack of brownies on the rim and then an ice cream sandwich on top of that. Sure, fun! But how in heck-fire am I supposed to even attempt eating that?! I can't say this one is smooth sailing to attack, or that you won't need a bib, but I can tell you that it holds up to epic proportions and is super fun to share with friends… and also holds up without any special riggings or duct tape! But don't be scared to get sticky fingers from all that delicious caramel.

For Cookie Sandwich:

- ▼ 2½ large Fudgy AF Brownies (page 36), divided
- ▼ 1½ Hotel Cookies (page 184), divided

For Shake:

- ▼ 2 tablespoons Silky Sunflower Caramel Sauce (page 52), plus more for the glass and for drizzling
- ▼ 1½ cups Very Vanilla Ice Cream (page 37), or store-bought vegan vanilla ice cream
- ▼ ½ cup (120 ml) unsweetened soy or almond milk
- ▼ 1 pinch sea salt
- ▼ Easy Whip 2 Ways, preferred variation (page 53), or store-bought vegan whipped cream
- ▼ Maldon sea salt (optional)

Chill a 12-ounce (355 ml) glass in the freezer for 30 minutes.

To make the cookie sandwich: Build a cookie sandwich with 1 cookie sandwiched between 2 brownies; set aside.

To make the shake: Put the ½ brownie and ½ cookie on a cutting board and use a sharp knife to chop both to bits, combining the bits and crumbles so they are mixed together.

Remove the glass from the freezer and use an offset spatula or butter knife to smear caramel in random spots on the inside of the glass. Then paint caramel along the top 1 inch (2.5 cm) of the outside edge of the glass as well as the rim. Roll the rim in the cookie-and-brownie crumble mixture until fully coated; if needed, use your hands to gently place more pieces on exposed spots of caramel.

Combine the ice cream, 2 tablespoons caramel, milk, and salt in a high-speed blender. Blend until smooth, 30 to 60 seconds, being careful not to over-blend.

Fill the chilled glass ¾ full with the shake and top with a large dollop of whipped cream so the whip comes up to the top of the glass.

Take the cookie sandwich and place it into the glass with a corner of the brownie down so that the two side corners of the diamond hold the brownie upright on the rim of the glass. Dollop whip everywhere possible, between the cookie and brownies and around the cookie sandwich. Drizzle with caramel. Sprinkle with any remaining cookie and brownie crumbs and Maldon sea salt, if using. Add a straw wherever you can squeeze it in!

Yield: 1 serving

Tip

The caramel may start to drip down the sides—this is great, use it! Smash more pieces of cookie and brownie into the dripping caramel. This will help it stay in place a bit and the more you have hanging out on the outside of the glass for this one the more epic it looks.

CINNAMON FRENCH TOAST SHAKE

Cinnamon Toast Crunch was my all-time favorite cereal as a kid. So much so that I created the Cinnamon Toast Granola in my last book, *The Simply Vegan Cookbook*, and now this! It's essentially a Cinnamon Toast Crunch milkshake with little pieces of French toast and whipped cream piled high. But if you just want a shake full of cinnamon goodness, skip the epic part and live your shake dreams!

For Mini French Toast Pieces:

▼ Cooking spray

▼ 1 batch Cake Batter (page 34)

▼ ¼ cup (55 g) vegan butter, melted

▼ 2 tablespoons (40 g) maple syrup

▼ 1 teaspoon ground cinnamon

For Shake:

▼ 1½ cups Very Vanilla Ice Cream (page 37), or store-bought vegan vanilla ice cream

▼ ½ cup (120 ml) unsweetened soy or almond milk

▼ ½ teaspoon ground cinnamon, plus more for garnish

▼ Easy Whip 2 Ways, preferred variation (page 53), or store-bought vegan whipped cream

▼ 2 cinnamon sticks, for garnish

▼ Maple syrup, for drizzling

To make the mini French toast pieces: Preheat the oven to 350°F (175°C, or gas mark 4). Line a 10 x 14-inch (26 x 36-cm) baking sheet with parchment paper and lightly spritz with cooking spray.

Pour half of the cake batter onto the prepared baking sheet and bake for 20 to 22 minutes, or until golden. See the box at right for ideas on how to use the remaining batter.

Let the cake cool for 10 minutes, then cut into ½-inch (1-cm) pieces to look like tiny pieces of toast. Increase the heat to 400°F (200°C, or gas mark 6).

In a large bowl, mix together the butter, maple syrup, and cinnamon.

Toss the pieces of toast with the butter mixture and return to the baking sheet. Bake for 5 minutes, toss with a spatula, and bake for an additional 5 minutes, or until the toast starts to brown and get crispy. Remove from the oven and let cool.

To make the shake: Chill a 12-ounce (355-ml) glass in the freezer for at least 30 minutes.

In a high-speed blender, combine the ice cream, milk, and cinnamon. Blend until smooth, 30 to 60 seconds, being careful not to over-blend. Fill the chilled glass with the shake, leaving 1 inch (2.5 cm) of space at the top.

Dollop enough whipped cream onto the top to fill the space and reach the top of the glass. Top with 4 to 6 French toast pieces, another layer of whip, another layer of French toast pieces, and so on, creating more layers, piling as high as possible. Stick the cinnamon sticks out the side of the whip, drizzle with the maple syrup, and sprinkle with more cinnamon, if desired.

Yield: 1 serving

Tip

There will be more than enough French toast pieces to make many shakes. The pieces will keep for up to 1 week stored in the refrigerator but will lose crispiness. Toss them onto a baking sheet and bake at 400°F (200°C, or gas mark 6) for 6 minutes, tossing once halfway through, until crispy again.

Extra Batter?

Use the remaining batter to make a single-layer 9-inch (23-cm) cake or 12 cupcakes, following the instructions on page 34, or make a second 10 x 14-inch (26 x 36-cm) cake to use in the Strawberry Short Shake on page 158. If not using the cake right away, wrap and freeze for up to 1 month, and thaw at room temp when ready to use. (Do not freezer batter.)

COFFEE AND DONUTS SHAKE

Dunkin' Donuts exists for a reason: Nothing beats the combination of donuts and coffee, except maybe a coffee shake and donuts! I encourage you to get creative with the donuts for this shake, using the chocolate glaze option and decorating with fun vegan sprinkles!

- ▶ 1½ cups Very Vanilla Ice Cream (page 37), or store-bought vegan vanilla ice cream

- ▶ ¾ cup (175 ml) cold brew or ¾ cup (175 ml) water with 1 teaspoon instant espresso dissolved in it

- ▶ 2 Crispy Cream Donuts (page 71), with traditional or chocolate glaze

- ▶ Easy Whip 2 Ways, preferred variation (page 153), or store-bought vegan whipped cream, (optional, see Tip)

Chill a 12-ounce (355 ml) glass in the freezer for at least 30 minutes.

Combine the ice cream and cold brew in a high-speed blender and blend for 30 to 60 seconds, until smooth. Pour into the chilled glass.

Set the 2 donuts on the rim of the glass, stacked on top of each other. Place a straw through the holes of the donuts. Use a piping bag, or resealable plastic bag with the tip of one corner cut off, to pipe the whipped cream (if using) into the holes until it fills to the top of the donuts.

Yield: 1 serving

Tip

The coconut whip tends to be heavier than the aquafaba whip; if you're using the coconut version, just be mindful to pipe it slowly into the donut holes so it sits on top of the shake and doesn't sink through right away.

BIRTHDAY CAKE SHAKE

I was deciding whether I actually wanted to tackle a book of this nature when I got on a plane and saw the cover of the inflight magazine picturing an outrageous shake—a birthday cake shake. I opened the magazine to an article focused on outrageous, over-the-top stunt foods. I took that moment as a sign, and I went forth to create this book, and this shake. This is the perfect single-serve specialty shake for the birthday person; everyone in attendance can have a piece of the cake that remains, but the celebrant gets cake and a shake!

For Birthday Cake:

▼ Cooking spray

▼ 1 batch Cake Batter (page 34)

▼ 1 batch Buttercream Frosting (page 34), ½ cup reserved for shake

▼ ½ to ¾ cup (112 to 168 g) vegan rainbow sprinkles, 1 tablespoon (14 g) reserved for shake

For Shake:

▼ ½ cup reserved Buttercream Frosting, divided

▼ 1½ cups Very Vanilla Ice Cream (page 37), or store-bought vegan vanilla ice cream

▼ ½ cup (120 ml) unsweetened soy or almond milk

▼ Easy Whip 2 Ways, preferred variation (page 53), or store-bought vegan whipped cream

▼ 1 tablespoon (14 g) reserved sprinkles

To make the birthday cake:
Preheat the oven to 350°F (175°C, or gas mark 4). Line two 7-inch (18-cm) round cake pans with parchment (see Tip on page 35) and lightly coat with cooking spray.

Use half of the cake batter to evenly fill each pan. Bake for 30 to 35 minutes, or until a toothpick inserted in the middle comes out clean. Let the cakes cool completely in the pans. See the box at right for ideas on how to use the remaining batter.

Remove the cakes from the pans, peel off the parchment, and cut off the domes of each cake to create flat tops. Frost the bottom layer of the cake. Top with the other layer of cake, and frost the top and sides completely. It doesn't have to be perfect, since you're adding sprinkles!

To sprinkle the cake:
Cut a piece of parchment paper about 4 inches (10 cm) wide and as tall as the cake. Lightly coat with cooking spray.

Pour the sprinkles (reserving 1 tablespoon) into an 8 x 8-inch (20 x 20-cm) baking pan, covering the bottom of the pan. Press the sprayed side of the parchment to the sprinkles so they adhere, then gently press the sprinkle side of the parchment to the side of the cake. Apply light pressure, rubbing up and down until all the sprinkles stick to the cake. Repeat until all sides of the cake are coated with sprinkles.

To make the shake:
Chill a 12-ounce (355-ml) glass in the freezer for 30 minutes.

Use an offset spatula or butter knife to paint the top 1 inch (2.5 cm) outside of the glass and the rim with a portion (about ¼ cup) of the reserved frosting. Roll the rim in the remaining 1 tablespoon (14 g) sprinkles until fully coated; if needed, use your hands to gently place more sprinkles on the exposed spots of frosting.

Combine the ice cream, the remaining ¼ cup frosting, and milk in a high-speed blender and blend for 30 to 60 seconds, until smooth. Fill the glass with the shake, leaving the top 1 inch of the glass empty.

Dollop 2 tablespoons (3 g) of whipped cream onto the top of the shake; it will be just enough to reach the top of the glass.

Cut the cake into 8 slices. Remove 1 slice and gently set it onto the glass with the frosted side on the rim and the pointed tip sitting on the opposite rim or dipping into the shake (don't fret, both are just as aesthetically pleasing). Dollop more whip around the sides of the cake and sprinkle with the remaining 1 tablespoon (14 g) sprinkles.

Place a candle in the top of the cake and a straw in the shake facing the opposite way of the candle.

Yield: 1 serving (plus 7 servings cake)

Tip

For assistance stabilizing the cake, use a straw: Slide the wider end of the cake down on a straw so the straw slides straight up into the cake. This step isn't completely necessary but helpful; a standard straw is short enough that it won't poke through the top of the cake so you can get the perfect picture for Instagram before you devour this tall glass of cake!

Extra Batter?

Use the remaining batter to make a single-layer 9-inch (23-cm) cake or 12 cupcakes, following the instructions on page 34, or make a 10 x 14-inch (26 x 36-cm) cake to use in the Strawberry Short Shake on page 158 or Cinnamon French Toast Shake on page 154. If not using the cake right away, wrap and freeze for up to 1 month, and thaw at room temp when ready to use. (Do not freezer batter.)

Pictured:
Coffee and Donuts Shake, Birthday Cake Shake, and Cinnamon French Toast Shake

STRAWBERRY SHORT SHAKE

I had a couple strawberry shortcake recipes I considered adding to this book, but they just didn't seem epic enough. I'm so in love with the flavors of it, though, that I couldn't resist making an epic shake out of it! This recipe will impress guests time after time. It's perfect for summer, when strawberries are in season, and you can easily prep it ahead by building your skewers to have ready in minutes (see Tip).

For Strawberries and Shortcake:

- ▶ Cooking spray
- ▶ 1 batch Cake Batter (page 34)
- ▶ 6 large strawberries
- ▶ Two 10-inch (25-cm) wooden skewers

For Shake:

- ▶ ¼ cup Buttercream Frosting (page 34)
- ▶ 1½ cups Very Vanilla Ice Cream (page 37), or store-bought vegan vanilla or strawberry ice cream
- ▶ 1 cup (145 g) fresh strawberries, hulled
- ▶ ½ cup (120 ml) unsweetened soy or almond milk
- ▶ Easy Whip 2 Ways, preferred variation (page 53), or store-bought vegan whipped cream

To make the strawberries and shortcake: Preheat the oven to 350°F (175°C, or gas mark 4). Line a 10 x 14-inch (26 x 36-cm) baking sheet with parchment paper and lightly coat with cooking spray.

Pour half of the cake batter onto the prepared baking sheet and bake for 18 to 20 minutes, or until a toothpick inserted in the middle comes out clean and the cake is golden brown. See the box at right for ideas on how to use the remaining batter.

Cool the cake completely. Meanwhile, chill a 12-ounce (355-ml) glass in the freezer for at least 30 minutes.

Cut the cake into 1½-inch (3.5-cm) squares. Set 11 of the squares aside for 1 shake, saving the rest for another time, or make shakes for 4 or 5 of your best friends now! Chop 4 of the 11 reserved squares into crumbly bits, and set aside.

Cut 3 strawberries into thirds so there is a bottom, middle, and top. Hull and thinly slice 2 of the strawberries. Cut a slit into the tip of the 1 remaining strawberry.

To make the shake: Remove the glass from the freezer and use an offset spatula or butter knife to paint the top 1 inch (2.5 cm) and the rim with the frosting. Roll the rim of the glass in the crumbled-up cake, pressing more cake into any exposed frosting.

In a high-speed blender, combine the ice cream, strawberries, and milk. Blend until smooth, 30 to 60 seconds, being careful not to over-blend. Pour into the chilled glass.

To build the skewers:

Place a skewer in the glass and skewer 1 square of cake, pushing it down so it rests on the rim. With a small spoon or piping bag, add a dollop of whipped cream onto the square, followed by the bottom of a strawberry. Add another piece of cake, another dollop of whip, then the middle piece of a strawberry. Add another piece of cake, another dollop of whip, then another middle piece of a strawberry. Add another piece of cake, then cut the skewer with kitchen shears so that only ¼ inch (6 mm) peeks up out of the cake. Add whip, then the top of a strawberry.

Place a second skewer in front of the assembled skewer. Add a square of cake, pushing it down so it rests on the rim, followed by a dollop of whip and the bottom piece of a strawberry. Add another piece of cake, more whip, and the final middle piece of strawberry. Add another piece of cake, and cut the top of the skewer with kitchen shears so that only ¼ inch (6 mm) peeks up out of the cake. Add whip and the top piece of a strawberry. This second skewer should be slightly shorter than the first.

Slide the remaining strawberry with a slit in the tip onto the rim of the glass in front of the skewers.

Dollop a generous amount of whip onto the top of the shake, stick a few strawberries slices in the whip, dollop again, and stick more strawberry slices in so that the sides of the slices are just peeking out. Sprinkle any remaining cake crumbles over the top. Add a straw (or two!) and enjoy.

Yield: 1 serving

Tip

To build the skewers in advance, leave the strawberry tops and the whip off, leaving some space between the cake and strawberries. When ready to assemble the entire shake, add the skewers to the glass and add the whip where needed on the skewers as directed, tightening up the spaces between the shortcake and the strawberries. Cut the tops off the skewers, add the strawberry tops, and finish building the shake as directed.

Extra Batter?

Use the remaining batter to make a single-layer 9-inch (23-cm) cake or 12 cupcakes, following the instructions on page 34, or make a second 10 x 14-inch (26 x 36-cm) cake for the next time you want to make this shake or the Cinnamon French Toast Shake on page 154. If not using the cake right away, wrap and freeze for up to 1 month, and thaw at room temp when ready to use. (Do not freezer batter.)

PUMPKIN CREAM CHEESE LATTE SHAKE

The pumpkin spiced latte and the cream cheese–stuffed pumpkin muffin are two coffee-chain classics that have become synonymous with the autumn season, so much so that I almost just named this shake "Autumn in a Glass," but I opted for those key words of "pumpkin," "cream cheese," and "latte" instead! You will see there are several bits and pieces to build this work of art; as with anything epic, it takes elements to create something big! I guarantee it's worth it, and you will have a bunch of cream cheese–stuffed muffins to hand out to your friends and family this fall when all is said and done (see Tip).

For Pumpkin Cupcakes:

- ▶ Cooking spray
- ▶ 1 batch Cake Batter (page 34), omitting ½ cup (120 ml) milk, 1 tablespoon (15 ml) vanilla extract, and the oil
- ▶ 1 cup (145 g) canned pumpkin puree (not pumpkin pie filling)
- ▶ 1 teaspoon pumpkin pie spice

For Cream Cheese Frosting:

- ▶ 1 batch Buttercream Frosting (page 34), omitting the shortening
- ▶ ½ cup (115 g) vegan cream cheese, room temperature

For Brown Sugar Pecans (optional):

- ▶ ½ cup (50 g) pecans, chopped
- ▶ 1 tablespoon (14 g) vegan butter, melted
- ▶ 1 tablespoon (15 g) organic dark brown sugar
- ▶ 1 pinch sea salt

For Shake:

- ▶ 1½ cups Very Vanilla Ice Cream (page 37), or store-bought vegan vanilla ice cream
- ▶ ½ cup (120 ml) cold brew or ½ cup (120 ml) milk with 1 teaspoon instant espresso dissolved in it
- ▶ 2 tablespoons (18 g) canned pumpkin puree (not pumpkin pie filling)
- ▶ ½ teaspoon pumpkin pie spice
- ▶ ¼ teaspoon ground cinnamon
- ▶ Easy Whip 2 Ways, preferred variation (page 53), or store-bought vegan whipped cream
- ▶ Cinnamon stick, for garnish

To make the pumpkin cupcakes: Preheat the oven to 350°F (175°C, or gas mark 4). Lightly coat two 12-cup muffin tins with cooking spray.

To make the cupcake batter, add the pumpkin puree and pumpkin pie spice to the cake batter. Mix well to combine.

Divide the batter among the muffin tins, filling the cavities ¾ to the top. Bake for 18 to 20 minutes, or until a toothpick in the center comes out clean. Let cool completely in the tins. Keep the oven on if making the pecans.

To make the cream cheese frosting: In place of the shortening, add the cream cheese to the frosting ingredients and make as directed. Chill for 1 hour while the cupcakes cool.

Meanwhile, chill a 12-ounce (355-ml) glass in the freezer for at least 30 minutes.

To make the brown sugar pecans (if using): With the oven still set to 350°F (175°C, or gas mark 4), line a baking sheet with parchment paper.

Combine the pecans, butter, brown sugar, and salt in a bowl and transfer to the prepared baking sheet, spreading out in one layer. Bake for 4 minutes. Toss the mixture around, spread back into a single layer, and bake for an additional 4 minutes, or until browned and fragrant. Remove from the oven and set aside to cool.

To make the shake: Remove the top (muffin top) from 1 cupcake. Quarter the top into equal-size pieces, and reserve. Chop the bottom of the cupcake into crumbly bits.

Remove the glass from the freezer and use an offset spatula or butter knife to paint the top 1 inch (2.5 cm) outside of the glass and the rim with the frosting. Roll the rim in the crumbled cupcake until fully coated; if needed, use your hands to gently place more cupcake crumbles on the exposed spots of frosting. Place brown sugar pecan pieces along the rim as well. Put the remaining frosting in a piping bag or a resealable plastic bag with a corner tip cut off.

Use a straw to poke a hole all the way through 1 cupcake; remove the straw. Slice that cupcake into thirds so there's a bottom, middle, and top. Place or pipe about 2 teaspoons (32 g) of frosting on the bottom layer, top with the middle piece of cupcake, and add about 2 teaspoons (32 g) of frosting on the middle piece. Top with the top piece of cupcake.

In a high-speed blender, combine the ice cream, coffee, pumpkin, pumpkin pie spice, and cinnamon. Blend until smooth, 30 to 60 seconds, being careful not to over-blend. Pour into the chilled glass.

Hold the layered cupcake on the rim with the hole part of it on the inside of the glass. Slide a straw through the middle of the hole in the cupcake until it reaches the bottom of the glass. The cupcake should sit on the rim with the help of the straw; if the straw sticks out the top, you can cut it down and dollop frosting over it to hide it.

Use a large dollop of whipped cream to fill the space between the cupcake and the rim of the glass. Stick the reserved quartered pieces of the muffin top into the whip. Add a cinnamon stick and a drinking straw, and sprinkle with the brown sugar pecans (if using).

Yield: 1 serving

Tip

What to do with all those extra tasty pumpkin cupcakes and frosting? Use a teaspoon to scoop out the center of each cupcake from the top and fill with frosting. If you have pecans left, sprinkle the cupcakes or stick a couple pieces onto the cream cheese part. Share with friends!

COOKIE DOUGH FROSTEE

Not quite a milkshake, but not ice cream either, it's America's beloved treat from that red-headed pigtailed minx, Wendy. If you've craved their Frosty and thought you wouldn't have it again since you went vegan, you thought wrong! Mix this up and enjoy, or take it to the epic level and pile that cookie dough on top. If you know someone going through a hard time (i.e., break up, etc.), this recipe does the trick. It's like a blast of nostalgia loaded into one cup, vegan style.

- ▼ ½ cup (120 ml) unsweetened soy or almond milk
- ▼ 1 tablespoon (5 g) unsweetened cocoa powder

- ▼ 1½ cups Very Vanilla Ice Cream (page 37), or store-bought vegan vanilla ice cream
- ▼ ½ cup Chocolate Chip Cookie Dough (page 33), chilled and crumbled

Chill a 12-ounce (355-ml) glass in the freezer for at least 30 minutes.

Combine the milk and cocoa powder in a high-speed blender. Blend until well combined. Add the ice cream and blend for 30 to 60 seconds, until smooth; it will be thicker than a milkshake. Pour into the chilled glass; it will come only ¾ way to the top.

Top with the crumbled cookie dough, gently dropping it in by small pieces so it doesn't sink to the bottom. Layer more on top until all the cookie dough is sitting nicely on top of the frostee.

Serve with a straw and a spoon.

Yield: 1 serving

Tip

Take it another step further and make it in the style of a Dairy Queen Blizzard! Put the frostee and cookie dough in a chilled bowl; mix until well combined. Transfer to a glass and serve with a spoon.

BLOOD ORANGE MIMOSA FLOAT

Mimosas are the stuff Sunday afternoons with friends are made of! I love to use blood oranges for mimosas because the flavors and aroma are stronger than a traditional orange. The deep red blush color of the blood orange is also beautiful, with a sexy and chic aesthetic. This float isn't just for those having a boozy Sunday Funday, however; swap out the booze (see Tip), so anyone can enjoy this tall drink of creamy, sweet, citrusy goodness!

- ▼ Juice of 2 blood oranges, 1 slice of orange reserved before juicing
- ▼ 2 scoops Very Vanilla Ice Cream (page 37), or store-bought vegan vanilla ice cream
- ▼ ¼ to ½ cup (60 to 120 ml) prosecco or Champagne (see Tip)

Chill a 16-ounce (470-ml) beer stein or mug in the freezer for 30 minutes.

Add the juice to the stein followed by the ice cream. Slowly top with the prosecco or Champagne. The prosecco will bubble up, so pour slowly to avoid overflow and wait a few seconds for

bubbles to subside before adding more. Serve with a straw and a spoon, with an orange slice with a slit cut in one side set on the rim for garnish.

Yield: 1 serving

Tip

To make an alcohol-free version of this ditty, simply swap out the booze for another bubbly like sparkling apple cider or ginger ale.

THE FANCY MARGA-REBA

I grew up listening to and was mildly fanatical about Country Queen/Legend, Reba McEntire. This drink is named after her and her hit song "Fancy." It's a mix of a little bit of spice, some sweetness, a touch of class, and a whole lot of sass—just like Reba herself. It's a super fun cocktail to serve in the summer months for a signature drink because everyone loves a margarita! Even more so, everyone loves a signature cocktail, especially a vibrant red one. Rename it for your party to suit your event, if you must, but I'm certain the Fancy Marga-Reba title will do just fine for any event.

For Citrus Rim and Garnish:

- ½ teaspoon sea salt
- ½ teaspoon orange zest
- 1 lime wedge
- 1 lime slice
- 1 orange slice

For Marga-Reba:

- Ice cubes
- 2 ounces (60 ml) high-quality tequila (see Tip)
- Juice of 1 orange
- Juice of 1½ limes
- 1 tablespoon (14 g) peeled and chopped beet
- 1 teaspoon agave
- ½ teaspoon minced ginger

To make the garnish: In a small bowl, combine the salt and zest, then transfer to a small plate.

Run the lime wedge around a rocks glass. Dip the rim in the salt mixture and roll around in the mixture until the entire rim is coated; fill with ice. Cut a slit in the lime and orange slices and place them on the rim of the glass with the orange slice behind the lime.

To make the Marga-Reba: In a high-speed blender, combine the tequila, orange juice, lime juice, beet, agave, and ginger. Blend until well combined and no bits of beet or ginger remain. Pour into the prepared glass.

Yield: 1 serving

Tip

Not drinking alone? Good for you, it's a party! Double, triple, or quadruple the recipe as needed to accommodate as many guests as you have, and please drink responsibly. For a nonalcoholic version, substitute the juice of 1 orange and 1 lime for the tequila.

SWEET EMOTIONS:
Donut Come for Me!
Sweets to Make Friends

CHAPTER 10

EPIC PB&J BARS

Peanut butter and jelly is a classic combo, am I right? But forget about the shenanigans with the bread for a minute and put the nostalgic PB&J flavors together in one pan! This is essentially a blondie brownie, topped with some sweet, sweet lip-smackin' raspberry preserves. (See Tip if you prefer a straight-up blondie; I'm told they have more fun.) And what a fun surprise treat to bring to a potluck for a dessert! These delightful squares are very rich and huge when cut into epic-servings size, so don't be hesitant to cut them smaller to create PB&J "bites" if preferred, see Tip.

- ▼ Cooking spray
- ▼ 2 cups (250 g) all-purpose flour
- ▼ 2 cups (450 g) packed organic light brown sugar
- ▼ 2 tablespoons (16 g) cornstarch
- ▼ 1 teaspoon baking powder
- ▼ 1 teaspoon sea salt
- ▼ 1½ cups (390 g or about a 16-ounce jar) creamy peanut butter (see Tip, page 182; same peanut butter rules apply)
- ▼ ¾ cup (177 ml) canola oil
- ▼ ½ cup (120 ml) unsweetened soy or almond milk
- ▼ 2 tablespoons (28 ml) vanilla extract
- ▼ 1½ cups (12-ounce/340-g jar) raspberry preserves

Preheat the oven to 350°F (175°C, or gas mark 4). Line a 9 x 13-inch (23 x 33-cm) baking pan with parchment paper and lightly coat with cooking spray.

In a large bowl, whisk together the flour, brown sugar, cornstarch, baking powder, and salt. Add the peanut butter, canola oil, milk, and vanilla; mix until well combined.

Spread the batter into the prepared pan, smoothing out evenly. Top with the raspberry preserves, spreading to create a smooth, even layer on top of the batter.

Bake for 45 to 50 minutes, or until the peanut butter batter starts to bubble up slightly in the middle under the preserves and the preserves are set and no longer jiggle.

Cool at room temperature for at least 1 hour, then transfer the entire pan to the refrigerator. Chill, uncovered, for an additional 2 hours before cutting. The longer you wait to cut into these, the better they will be! Because of the excessive amount of peanut butter that makes these epic, they can be fragile when cut too early. You have been warned; cut into 12 bars with caution.

Yield: 12 epic bars

Tip

Make these blondies! Omit the raspberry preserves, mix in ½ cup (350 g) vegan chocolate chips, and add a sprinkle of Maldon sea salt to the top of the batter before baking as directed. Or make them PB&J "bites" by cutting each large bar into quarters. To speed up the cooling process, see the Tip on page 185.

CARAMEL-STUFFED COOKIES 'N CREAM CUPCAKES

Oreos are vegan. Yes, I said it. They make the PETA list of "vegan foods that will surprise you" every year, and many a vegan around the world enjoys them, often. Don't feel you have to use Oreo cookies for success in this recipe, however. Feel free to bake smaller versions of the Chocolate Chip Cookies on page 33, or use one of the many vegan brands of cookies on the market for this recipe. The caramel in the middle adds that extra touch to make this truly epic and also provides your guests with a delightful surprise when they take a bite!

▼ 1 batch Cake Batter (page 34)

▼ 1 package (14.3 ounces/405 g) Oreo cookies or 36 similar cookies of choice

▼ 1 batch Silky Sunflower Caramel Sauce (page 52)

▼ 1 batch Buttercream Frosting (page 34) (see Tip)

Preheat the oven to 350°F (175°C, or gas mark 4). Line two 12-cup muffin tins with paper liners, or bake in two batches if you have only one muffin tin.

Put 1 tablespoon of batter in each liner. Place 1 cookie flat on top of the batter, then add enough batter on the top of the cookie to fill the liner ¾ full.

Bake for 18 to 22 minutes, or until the tops start to turn a golden brown and a toothpick inserted into one comes out clean. Repeat as needed until all the batter is baked.

Let cupcakes cool for 10 minutes, then remove from the pan to cool completely. Repeat with the remaining batter.

From the top of a cupcake, scoop a heaping teaspoon out of the center. Fill the hole with 1 heaping teaspoon of caramel. Repeat with the remaining cupcakes.

Put the remaining Oreos in a resealable plastic bag and seal it, making sure all the air is released. Use a rolling pin to crush the Oreos until they've all been crumbled to bits.

Spread or pipe 1 tablespoon (18 g) of frosting on each cupcake, drizzle with caramel, and sprinkle with the Oreo crumbles.

Yield: 24 cupcakes

Tip

Piping the frosting onto the cupcakes adds that extra-special touch, and I'm all about it—get fancy! But know that you will likely have just enough frosting for all 24 cupcakes using 1 tablespoon (18 g) each. Pipe with caution, keeping the amount per cupcake in mind, or make a double batch of frosting to pipe with zero constraints.

DOUBLE-STACKED COOKIE DOUGH CAKE

This is the Daddy Warbucks of cakes because it's rich AF. Truth. It's the cake you make for the cookie-dough lover in your life on their birthday. It's one of those things you bite into and say, "Ohmigod … I can't possibly take another bite, it's so rich," but then you suddenly can't stop taking bite after bite! The baked cookies put your garnish game on top and make this truly epic.

For Cake:

- ▼ Canola oil or cooking spray
- ▼ 1 batch Cake Batter (page 34)
- ▼ 1 batch Chocolate Chip Cookie Dough (page 33), divided

For Frosting:

- ▼ 1 cup (225 g) vegan butter, room temperature
- ▼ ½ cup (115 g) packed organic light brown sugar
- ▼ 1 tablespoon (5 g) unsweetened cocoa powder
- ▼ 1 teaspoon molasses
- ▼ 3½ cups (420 g) organic confectioners' sugar

To make the cake: Preheat the oven to 350°F (175°C, or gas mark 4). Lightly coat 2 round 9-inch (23-cm) cake pans with canola oil or cooking spray and line with parchment paper (see Tip on page 35).

Divide the batter evenly into the prepared pans. Bake for 30 to 35 minutes, or until a toothpick inserted in the middle comes out clean.

Let the cakes cool completely in the pans.

To make the cookie dough: Preheat the oven to 375°F (190°C, or gas mark 5). Line a baking sheet with parchment paper.

Spread 2 cups (550 g) of the cookie dough in an 8 x 8-inch (20 x 20-cm) baking dish; it doesn't have to be smooth across the top, just evenly dispersed. Place in the freezer for at least 30 minutes to solidify, but not long enough to freeze solid (transfer to the refrigerator, if need be, until ready to use).

Place the remaining dough, 1 rounded tablespoon (about 20 g) at a time, on the prepared baking sheet, leaving 2 inches (5 cm) between the dough balls. Bake for 9 to 11 minutes, or until the edges of the cookies have browned. This may need to be done in 2 batches depending on the size of your baking sheet; you will have 18 cookies. Remove from the oven and transfer to a cooling rack to cool completely.

To make the frosting: In a large bowl with a hand mixer, or the bowl of a stand mixer fitted with the paddle attachment, cream together the butter, brown sugar, cocoa powder, and molasses on medium speed until smooth and creamy, about 2 minutes. On low speed, add the confectioners' sugar, 1 cup (120 g) at a time, mixing until well incorporated and a creamy frosting texture has formed.

To build the cake: Crumble the chilled cookie dough into chunks.

Remove the cakes from the pans, peel off the parchment, and cut off the domes of each cake to create flat tops. Set the bottom layer of the cake on a cake plate or serving tray. Top with a large dollop of frosting and spread to the edges with an offset spatula or butter knife. Place 1 cup of the raw cookie dough crumbles on top of the frosted bottom layer, and then set 12 baked cookies flat on the top of the cookie dough.

Place the second cake layer on top and frost the cake until completely covered with the remaining frosting. Halve the remaining 6 cookies and place them on the perimeter of the top of the cake with the round side sticking up and the cut side sticking into the cake so it stands upright. Add the remaining raw cookie dough to the top of the cake, in the center of the baked cookies.

To serve, cut the cake into 12 slices; each piece should have ½ of a baked cookie sticking out of the top.

Yield: 12 servings

Tip

Don't let this cake intimidate you. Make all the components the day before, or even the morning of, then place it all in the fridge and forget about it. When you come back to assemble the cake, it will seem less overwhelming than doing it all at once, and everything will have cooled sufficiently.

MATCHA MINT POPS WITH PISTACHIO CRUNCH SHELL

I dedicate these pops to America's Vegan Sweetheart, Chloe Coscarelli. Chloe has been a friend and mentor ever since I started my journey into the culinary world, and she has inspired my work ethic and passion for simple but creative cooking for the masses! When I think of cooking with Chloe, I think of two things: avocados and matcha! I've got so matcha love for you Chloe, these ones are for you.

For Pops:

- ▼ 1 can (13.5 ounces/983 ml) full-fat unsweetened coconut milk
- ▼ ½ cup (89 g) pitted Medjool dates
- ▼ ⅓ cup (45 g) cashews, soaked in water overnight or boiled for 10 minutes and drained
- ▼ 2 tablespoons (28 ml) agave
- ▼ 1 tablespoon (15 ml) vodka (optional, see Tip, page 37)
- ▼ 1 teaspoon vanilla extract
- ▼ 1 teaspoon peppermint extract
- ▼ 1½ teaspoons matcha powder

For Coconut Crackle Shell:

- ▼ 1 batch Crackle and Fudgy Chocolate Sauce, crackle version (page 51) (see Tip)
- ▼ ½ cup (62 g) pistachios, shelled and crushed

In a high-speed blender, combine the coconut milk, dates, cashews, agave, vodka (if using), vanilla, peppermint, and matcha. Blend until smooth and creamy. Transfer to six (3-ounce/90 ml) ice-pop molds and freeze overnight.

Line a baking sheet, small enough to fit in the freezer, with parchment paper.

Set up a work station with the freshly made chocolate sauce in a bowl, the crushed pistachios on a plate, and the lined baking sheet nearby.

Take the pops out of their molds (if difficult to remove, run briefly under warm water to loosen them up), and one by one hold a pop over the chocolate sauce and use a spoon to drizzle desired amount of sauce all over it. Quickly dip it in the pistachios, coating it all over, then place it on the baking sheet. Repeat with the remainder, moving quickly so the pops don't melt. When finished, enjoy immediately or place in the freezer to enjoy later. Finished pops will last up to 2 weeks in a tightly sealed container or wrapped in plastic wrap in the freezer.

Yield: 6 pops

Tip

To get that crackle shell just right, you need the frozen pops to meet the fresh crackly sauce, so don't make the crackle sauce until you're ready to drizzle the pops. Not a fan of pistachios? Coat these bad boys with anything you like, including coconut flakes, cake sprinkles, crushed graham crackers, mini marshmallows, or your preferred nut or seed!

I TRY TO THINK ABOUT ELVIS ICE CREAM

Elvis is in the building! Or at least, this tasty version of Elvis-inspired ice cream is in the building. Utilizing those smoky Quinoa Bacon Bits on page 14, with the addition of bananas in the base, delivers a creamy and luscious texture and flavor. This ice cream is legit; I love it so much that when I'm having a bad day, I just close my eyes and try to think about Elvis … ice cream. And before I know it I'm home sweet home with a Churro Cup Sundae (page 172), filled with this ice cream, and a smile on my face.

- ▼ 1 batch Very Vanilla Ice Cream base (page 37), omitting the water and vanilla

- ▼ 2 ripe bananas

- ▼ 1 cup Quinoa Bacon Bits (page 14)

- ▼ ½ cup (130 g) creamy peanut butter, divided (see Tip, page 182; same peanut butter rules apply)

Freeze the ice cream maker base according to the manufacturer's instructions; for most brands, it's overnight before making the ice cream.

In a high-speed blender, combine all the ingredients for the Very Vanilla Ice Cream, replacing the water and vanilla with the bananas. Blend for about 2 minutes, until smooth and creamy. Transfer to a container, cover, and let chill in the refrigerator for 3 hours.

Transfer the mixture to the ice cream maker and follow the manufacturer's instructions. When the ice cream begins to thicken and is almost to the point of stiffening up, add the bacon bits. Churn until desired consistency is reached according to the manufacturer's instructions.

Transfer the ice cream to a loaf pan in 3 layers. Add the first layer of ice cream followed by half of the peanut butter, dropped by the spoonful in different spots of the ice cream; use a butter knife to swirl the peanut butter around. Add another layer of ice cream and the remaining peanut butter, using the same technique to swirl the peanut butter and evenly disperse it. Add the last bit of ice cream for the final layer and smooth it out.

Wrap tightly with plastic wrap, pressing the wrap onto the ice cream to eliminate air from the mixture and prevent ice crystals from forming. Freeze overnight.

Yield: about 1 quart (1,037 g)

Tip

Homemade ice creams don't have the shelf life of store-bought ice creams because they aren't full of additives and stabilizers. For this reason, it's best to enjoy the ice creams in this book within 2 weeks. However, if you know you won't be able to eat a quart of ice cream that quickly, add ¼ teaspoon xanthan gum when blending the ingredients in the first step. Xanthan, a powdered derivative of corn, will help reduce ice crystals, thicken, and stabilize when you're saving your batch of homemade goodness for a rainy day!

CHURRO CUP SUNDAES

Churros are just the best! And turning them into a bowl so I can spoon up a bite full of caramel sauce, ice cream, and crunchy churro is a dream come true. Don't feel stuck to these guidelines for a sundae, though; this recipe is all about the churro cup, and I merely suggest a fairly straightforward traditional sundae. But get crazy in that kitchen of yours! Build the sundae of your own dreams with this perfectly round and crisp churro bowl as the base.

For Churro Cups:

- ▼ 1 cup (235 ml) water
- ▼ ¼ cup (55 g) vegan butter
- ▼ ¼ cup (38 g) organic light brown sugar
- ▼ 1 teaspoon sea salt
- ▼ 2 cups (250 g) all-purpose flour
- ▼ 2 teaspoons (10 ml) vanilla extract
- ▼ ½ cup (100 g) organic cane sugar
- ▼ 1 teaspoon ground cinnamon
- ▼ Cooking spray

For Sundaes:

- ▼ I Try to Think About Elvis Ice Cream (page 171), or vegan ice cream of choice
- ▼ Crackle and Fudgy Chocolate Sauce, preferred variation (page 51)
- ▼ Silky Sunflower Caramel Sauce (page 52)
- ▼ Easy Whip 2 Ways, preferred variation (page 53), or store-bought vegan whipped cream
- ▼ 4 maraschino cherries, dye-free if possible (optional)
- ▼ Brown Sugar Pecans (page 160, optional)

In a large saucepan, bring the water, butter, brown sugar, and salt to a boil, stirring to dissolve the sugar. Remove from the heat. Add the flour and vanilla, stirring with a wooden spoon until it all comes together as a dough that's free of lumps. Cool for 15 minutes. Transfer ¼ of the batter to a piping bag without a tip or a resealable plastic bag with a hole the size of a dime cut off one of the corners.

Preheat the oven to 425°F (220°C, or gas mark 7), and invert a 12-cup muffin tin.

Create a bowl by piping the batter around one of the inverted cavities. Start piping from the bottom, making sure the batter stays connected. Each level of batter should be touching; if there are holes, the cup will not hold its structure. The tops should be covered completely with batter as well.

Repeat, filling the bag with another portion of batter for another cup, and choosing a muffin cavity that isn't next to the first one, so the cups won't touch when they bake. Once all 4 are piped onto the tin, run a finger along the sides of the cups to ensure all the batter is sticking together, and use any remaining batter to fill in holes and gaps. Make sure the top portion, which will become the bottom of the cup, is flat so it will sit level when creating the sundae.

Bake for 14 to 16 minutes, or until dry and firm. Cool for 8 to 10 minutes, until cool enough to handle, then use a butter knife to pop the cups off the pan.

In a small bowl, combine the cane sugar and cinnamon. Spray a churro cup lightly on the inside and outside with cooking spray. Transfer the cup to the sugar mixture and gently turn it around in the mixture on its sides until completely coated. Sprinkle some sugar mixture on the inside of the cup and gently shake around until the insides are completely coated. Repeat with the remaining cups.

Add 1 large scoop of ice cream to the churro bowl and top with the chocolate sauce, caramel, whipped cream, a cherry, and pecans (if using).

Yield: 4 servings

Tip

This batter is thick like a dough and requires some muscle to push out of the piping bag. If you're using a resealable plastic bag for piping, double up so the baggie doesn't break. If you are making sundaes for fewer than 4 people, stack the bowls on each other for a double-stack sundae. Churros are best when made fresh, so no better time than the present to gobble these up!

S'MORES COOKIE CUPS

Who doesn't love s'mores!? The only issue I have ever had with these delicious campfire delights is the marshmallow and chocolate oozing everywhere. While messy is fun (I'm totally into it), I can't help but remember a camping trip in my teens where we were ill-prepared to clean up after the s'mores enjoyment, and we were left with sticky hands and faces for the night. Hopefully these cups take just a bit of the mess out of the equation, but I can't promise all of it!

▼ Canola oil or cooking spray

▼ 6 vegan graham cracker sheets

▼ 1 batch Chocolate Chip Cookie Dough (page 33)

▼ Crackle and Fudgy Chocolate Sauce, crackle version (page 51)

▼ 24 large vegan marshmallows

Preheat the oven to 375°F (190°C, or gas mark 5). Lightly coat two 12-cup muffin tins with canola oil or cooking spray, or bake in two batches if you have only one muffin tin.

Prepare the graham crackers by breaking each piece into 1-inch (2.5-cm) squares; you should get 8 pieces per graham cracker sheet. Quick hack: Snap the crackers apart where they are perforated and then cut those pieces into quarters with a knife for more uniform pieces.

Fill each muffin cavity with 2 tablespoons (40 g) cookie dough and bake for 8 minutes. Remove from the oven and push 2 pieces of graham cracker, edge first, into the top near the side of the cookie. Stack 2 more pieces of graham cracker together, lay them flat side down in the middle of the cookie, and push them about ½ inch (1 cm) down into the cookie; the edges of the cookie will come up a little bit.

Add ½ teaspoon of the chocolate sauce over the flat graham crackers. Lay a marshmallow lengthwise on top of the chocolate-covered flat graham pieces and press down again slightly; the cookie will rise up on the outsides a little more. Repeat with the remaining ingredients.

Return to the oven and bake for 8 minutes, or until the marshmallows have just started to turn brown; they'll puff up but will deflate a little when cooling.

Cool 15 minutes, pop out of the pan with a soft spatula, and lightly drizzle with more chocolate sauce.

Yield: 2 dozen cookies

Tip

If taking these cookies to an event, set in the freezer for 1 hour, then drizzle the cold cookies with the Crackle and Fudgy Chocolate Sauce; it will seize on the cookies, so you have less of a mess to travel with! (They should be served at room temperature, though, not cold.) Also, vegan graham crackers do exist, I promise; be diligent when reading labels.

SNEAKY PICKLE PINEAPPLE ICE CREAM

It's weird, right? Pickle ice cream. I thought so too, but all of New York was going crazy over some place having a pickle soft serve that I wasn't able to have because it had dairy. So I went about creating my own! I wasn't a fan of just the pickle, but once I added the pineapple and caramel, I couldn't stop eating it! The combination of salty and sweet with the luscious silky caramel won me over.

- ▶ 1 batch Very Vanilla Ice Cream base (page 37), omitting the water

- ▶ 1 cup (235 ml) pickle juice from a jar of pickles

- ▶ 1 cup (165 g) fresh, canned, or frozen roughly chopped pineapple

- ▶ ½ cup Silky Sunflower Caramel Sauce, divided (page 52)

Freeze the ice cream maker base according to the manufacturer's instructions; for most brands, it's overnight before making the ice cream.

In a high-speed blender, combine the pickle juice and all the ingredients for the ice cream base (minus the water). Blend until smooth, 1 to 2 minutes. Transfer to a container, cover, and refrigerate for at least 3 hours.

Transfer the mixture to the ice cream maker and follow the manufacturer's instructions. When the ice cream has started to firm up and is almost done churning, add the pineapple and let it continue to churn until the pineapple is well incorporated.

Transfer the ice cream to a loaf pan in 3 layers. Add the first layer of ice cream followed by half of the caramel sauce, dropped by the spoonful in different spots of the ice cream; use a butter knife to swirl the caramel around. Add another layer of ice cream and the remaining caramel, using the same technique to swirl the caramel and evenly disperse it. Top with a final layer of ice cream and smooth it out.

Wrap tightly with plastic wrap, pressing the wrap onto the ice cream to eliminate air from the mixture and prevent ice crystals from forming. Freeze overnight.

Yield: about 1 quart (1,062 g)

Tip

Cut a fresh pineapple in half lengthwise and gut the insides; put 3 large scoops of this ice cream in the pineapple boat and top with caramel, Crackle and Fudgy Chocolate Sauce (page 51), and some Easy Whip 2 Ways (page 53), or store-bought vegan whipped cream for a decadent sundae served up in a fun boat! Add tiki umbrellas, bananas, and chopped nuts to turn your sundae game on strong for a Banana Split Pineapple Pirate Ship!

KALE ME CRAZY ICE CREAM

Who knew getting your greens in could taste so good? Take the Very Vanilla Ice Cream from the basics chapter (page 37) and just toss in some kale, cherries, and chocolate chips for an ice cream all of your buddies will be green with envy for! This bright green base is not only super tasty, but is also a great conversation piece at parties.

- ▼ 1 batch Very Vanilla Ice Cream base (page 37)
- ▼ 1 cup (67 g) chopped kale
- ▼ 1 cup (155 g) frozen sweet cherries, roughly chopped (see Tip)
- ▼ 1 cup (175 g) mini vegan chocolate chips

Freeze the ice cream maker base according to the manufacturer's instructions; for most brands, it's overnight before making the ice cream.

Make the ice cream base in a high-speed blender as directed, adding the kale. Blend until smooth and green. Transfer the base to a container with a lid and refrigerate for 3 hours.

Transfer the mixture to the ice cream maker and prepare according to manufacturer's instructions. When the ice cream has started to thicken up, add the cherries and chocolate chips and continue to churn until evenly dispersed and the ice cream has reached a soft serve consistency. Transfer to a container, seal tightly, and freeze overnight.

Yield: about 1 quart (1,217 g)

Tip

It will be tempting to thaw the cherries first to make it easier to chop them, but doing so will make the cherries juicy and turn your green ice cream red; avoid the temptation and put some muscle into chopping those frozen cherries.

Pictured:
I Try to Think About Elvis, Kale Me Crazy, Sneaky Pickle Pineapple, and The Hotel Cookie Ice Cream Sandwich

POWER TOWER BROWNIE SUNDAE

The Dairy Queen brownie sundae, the brownie bottom pie from Bennigan's, the brownie cheesecake at The Cheesecake Factory ... the list goes on. People love a brownie because it usually holds some sort of nostalgic "fresh-baked homemade" feeling—but also because it's a piece of cake you can eat with your hands! I don't suggest digging into this outrageous tower with your hands, but I certainly wouldn't judge you for it either. The parts are simple, but the build is impressive and epic, and it's the perfect dessert to share for up to 6 or even 8 people! Decadent and delicious, ice cream and brownies never came together so well.

▼ 3 Fudgy AF Brownies (page 36)

▼ 1 cup Very Vanilla Ice Cream (page 37), or store-bought vegan vanilla ice cream, divided

▼ One 10-inch (25-cm) wooden skewer (optional)

▼ Crackle and Fudgy Chocolate Sauce, fudgy version (page 51)

▼ Silky Sunflower Caramel Sauce (page 52)

▼ Easy Whip 2 Ways, preferred variation (page 53), or store-bought vegan whipped cream

▼ Sweet Chili Cocktail Peanuts (page 80), chopped

▼ 1 maraschino cherry, dye-free if possible

Build the sundae in a bowl with 1 brownie as the base followed by half of the ice cream. Top with another brownie and the remaining ice cream. Top with the final brownie. If desired for stability, pierce a skewer through the middle down to the bottom; cut the top off so only ¼ inch (6 mm) is sticking out.

Top with the chocolate sauce, caramel, a large dollop of whipped cream, peanuts, and a cherry.

Serve immediately with spoons for sharing!

Yield: 6 to 8 servings

Tip

The skewer isn't necessary, but it is helpful if you want to take time dressing up the tower with sauces and accouterments. Or if you want to pause to take a good picture for your social media, the skewer helps hold the brownies in place when the ice cream gets a little soft. It also helps hold everything in place when you dig in with a spoon! Just be sure to warn your sharing buddies of the skewer in the middle.

CAPTAIN CHOW DONUTS WITH SALTY PEANUT BUTTER FILLING

The donut game in the vegan world is STRONG. That being said, I'm not trying to reinvent the wheel! But I am more than happy to offer this concoction to you, with a spin on the traditional "puppy chow" (a party favorite of sugar-coated Chex cereal, chocolate chips, and peanut butter). Borrowing the Salty Peanut Butter Frosting from the Pad Thai Cupcakes on page 182, the combination is an arranged marriage for the books! It's an "OMG! No you didn't!" kind of donut, and I hope you love it as much as the #epicvegan test kitchen does!

For Captain Chow:

- 2 tablespoons (28 g) vegan butter
- ½ cup (87 g) vegan chocolate chips
- ¼ cup (65 g) creamy peanut butter
- ½ teaspoon vanilla extract
- 4 cups (144 g) Cap'n Crunch cereal or favorite crunchy vegan rice-square cereal
- ¾ cup (90 g) organic confectioners' sugar

For Donuts:

- 1 batch Crispy Cream Donuts dough (page 71), proofed and ready to be turned out
- Canola oil
- 1 batch Peanut Butter Frosting (page 182)
- 2 batches Chocolate Glaze (page 71)
- 1 teaspoon unsweetened soy or almond milk (optional)

To make the captain chow:

Melt the butter in a medium saucepan over low heat. Add the chocolate chips, peanut butter, and vanilla. Stir until well combined and melted. Remove from the heat.

In a large bowl, combine the cereal with the chocolate mixture and toss until all the cereal is coated. Add the confectioners' sugar and toss again until all the cereal is coated. Cover the bowl and place in the freezer for 30 minutes, then transfer to the refrigerator until needed.

To make the donuts: On a lightly floured surface, roll out the dough into a 9 x 12-inch (23 x 30-cm) rectangle, ½ inch (1 cm) thick; do not overwork the dough. Cut into 12 squares that are 3 x 3 inches (7.5 x 7.5 cm) in size. Separate the squares, leaving 1 inch (2.5 cm) of space between them. Cover with a clean kitchen towel and let rest for 30 minutes, or until doubled in size.

In a large skillet, pour 1 inch (2.5 cm) of canola oil. Heat the oil to 350°F (175°C) when tested with a candy thermometer or until bubbles form around the handle of a wooden spoon when inserted into the oil. Line a plate with paper towels.

Gently transfer the donuts to the oil, 2 or 3 at a time. Fry on one side for 15 to 25 seconds, until golden, then flip with tongs and fry an additional 15 to 25 seconds, or until golden. Transfer to the paper towel–lined plate or a cooling rack; cool completely.

Fill a piping bag with a round tip with the frosting. Use a paring knife to cut a small slit in the end of a donut. Carefully slide the knife inside the donut to separate the dough on the inside and make room for the filling. Stick the pastry bag tip in the hole and gently fill the donut with about 1 tablespoon (18 g) of frosting, until it's heavier in weight. Be careful not to overfill, as the donut could break and filling will ooze out of either side. Be judicious in using the frosting to be sure you make it to the last donut with enough filling for all.

Take the Captain Chow out of the refrigerator and have ready nearby. Ice 1 donut with 1 tablespoon (22 g) of the glaze and dip it into the bowl of chow. Pull the donut out of the chow and use your free hand to gently push the pieces of chow into the glaze to adhere them to the donut. Set aside and continue with the remaining donuts.

Add the milk to the remaining glaze to loosen it up, if needed, to make it drizzleable. Drizzle over the top of the chow on the donuts. Let the donuts sit for 15 minutes for the chocolate to dry.

Yield: 12 donuts

Tip

It's imperative to use a piping bag to fill donuts; the DIY approach with a resealable plastic bag won't work here. But that's okay! If you don't have a piping bag, there's already a lot happening here; just skip the filling, and it will still be all sorts of epic. If you have any leftover Captain Chow, bring that to the party to pass around too; it will be gone faster than you can say, "Donut worry! Be vegan!"

PAD THAI CUPCAKES

When I was filming my series *The Vegan Roadie*, I had the pleasure of visiting a place called Lulu's Local Eatery in St. Louis, Missouri. They had so many delicious items on the menu, but I will never forget this cupcake outsourced from an independent baker by the name of Stimulus Baking Company created by Lauren Wamhoff. In the past, when re-creating this cupcake, I've used tamarind concentrate to really get those pad thai flavors, but I found the combination of soy and lime does the trick! This is a perfect addition to any party to get your guests talking.

For Cupcakes:

- ▼ 1 cup (235 ml) unsweetened soy or almond milk
- ▼ 1 teaspoon apple cider vinegar
- ▼ 1¼ cups (157 g) all-purpose flour
- ▼ ¾ cup (150 g) organic cane sugar
- ▼ 2 tablespoons (16 g) cornstarch
- ▼ ¾ teaspoon baking powder
- ▼ ½ teaspoon baking soda
- ▼ ½ teaspoon sea salt
- ▼ ⅓ cup (59 ml) canola oil
- ▼ 2 teaspoons (10 ml) vanilla extract
- ▼ 1 teaspoon soy sauce
- ▼ Juice of 1 lime
- ▼ 2 tablespoons (30 ml) Sweet Thai Chili Sauce (page 46), or store-bought sweet Thai chili sauce
- ▼ 6 lime wedges, cut in half (see Tip)
- ▼ Chopped peanuts (optional)

For Peanut Butter Frosting:

- ▼ ¼ cup (65 g) creamy peanut butter
- ▼ ¼ cup (55 g) vegan butter
- ▼ 2 cups (240 g) organic confectioners' sugar
- ▼ 1 tablespoon (15 ml) plus 1 teaspoon (5 ml) soy sauce
- ▼ 1 tablespoon (15 ml) unsweetened soy or almond milk

To make the cupcakes:

Preheat the oven to 350°F (175°C, or gas mark 4). Line a 12-cup muffin tin with cupcake liners.

In a small bowl, mix together the milk and apple cider vinegar; set aside for 5 minutes, or until thickened.

In a large bowl, whisk together the flour, sugar, cornstarch, baking powder, baking soda, and salt. Add the canola oil, vanilla, soy sauce, lime juice, and the milk-and-cider mixture. Whisk until well combined and there are fewer lumps, but do not overmix.

Fill each cupcake liner ¾ full. Bake for 20 to 22 minutes, or until a toothpick inserted in the middle of one comes out clean. Remove from the oven and cool completely on a cooling rack while making the frosting.

To make the frosting: In a bowl with a hand mixer, or in a stand mixer fitted with the paddle attachment, cream together the peanut butter and butter on medium speed. Add the confectioners' sugar, soy sauce, and milk; mix until smooth and creamy but still slightly firm.

Once the cupcakes have cooled, frost as desired, with a piping bag or with a good ol' fashioned butter knife. Drizzle the top of each cupcake with ½ teaspoon chili sauce, place half a lime wedge into the top of the frosting, and sprinkle with chopped peanuts (if using).

When serving, instruct guests to squeeze their lime over the top of the cupcake for the full pad thai experience!

Yield: 12 cupcakes

Tip

This is frosting; I find I get best results with the "creamy" style peanut butters that don't fall under the "natural" label. If you rely on the "natural" label, just be aware that the oil content will affect the fluffiness and firmness of the frosting. For the lime garnish, cut a lime in half lengthwise, then slice into half-moons (lime wedges); cut the half-moons in half, and you have a small lime wedge perfect for the top of this cupcake.

THE HOTEL COOKIE ICE CREAM SANDWICH

There is a certain hotel that gives their guests chocolate chip cookies upon check-in. This cookie is so decadent, rich, and delicious—and they always serve it warm to boot! These cookies are so good that I would ignore the "upon check-in only" cookie policy and walk up and get one every time I went through the lobby back in my nonvegan days. Gluttony at its finest! This is my version of that cookie.

- 2 tablespoons (14 g) flax meal
- ¼ cup (60 ml) water
- 1 cup (225 g) vegan butter
- ¾ cup (170 g) packed organic light brown sugar
- ¾ cup (150 g) organic cane sugar
- 2¼ cups (282 g) all-purpose flour
- ½ cup (50 g) oat flour (see Tip)
- 1½ teaspoons baking soda
- 1 teaspoon sea salt
- ½ teaspoon ground cinnamon
- 1 tablespoon (15 ml) vanilla extract
- Juice of ½ lemon
- 1½ cups (175 g, or one 10-ounce bag) vegan mini chocolate chips (use regular size, if desired)
- 1 cup (120 g) chopped walnuts
- 1 batch Very Vanilla Ice Cream (page 37), or 3 cups store-bought vegan vanilla ice cream

Preheat the oven to 400°F (200°C, or gas mark 6). Line a baking sheet with parchment paper. (If you have 2 sheets, use them.)

Combine the flax with water and set aside for 5 minutes, until thickened.

In a large bowl with a hand mixer, or in a stand mixer fitted with the paddle attachment, cream together the butter, brown sugar, and cane sugar until smooth. Add the flax mixture, all-purpose flour, oat flour, baking soda, salt, cinnamon, vanilla, and lemon juice. Mix on medium speed until well combined. Add the chocolate chips and walnuts, and mix until equally dispersed throughout the dough.

Measure out 3 tablespoons (66 g) of dough and create a ball. Transfer to the prepared baking sheet and gently flatten with the palm of your hand. Repeat with the remaining cookie dough, leaving 2 inches (5 cm) of space between each cookie. You will likely need to bake them in 2 batches.

Bake for 8 minutes, rotate the baking sheet, and bake an additional 7 minutes, or until the cookies have spread and browned on the edges. Remove from the oven, carefully transfer to a cooling rack, and cool completely. Freeze for 1 hour before making the ice cream sandwiches.

Let the ice cream set out at room temperature for 5 to 10 minutes, until it's easily scooped from the container. Using a ½ cup measuring cup, scoop the ice cream onto the flat side of a cookie, then top with the bottom side of another cookie and smoosh down to spread the ice cream. Repeat with the remaining cookies. Freeze sandwiches until ready to serve.

Sandwiches can be frozen for up to 1 month when wrapped in plastic or stored in a sealed container, but best when served within 2 weeks.

Yield: 6 servings

Tip

If you don't have oat flour, simply create your own by processing ½ cup (40 g) rolled oats in a food processor or high-speed blender until ½ cup fine meal is formed.

SWEET 'N SALTY BOOKMARK BARS

I call these Bookmark Bars because you will need to bookmark three recipes in the first couple chapters to make them. This is a combination sensation of sweet, gooey brownie topped with chocolate chips, tart dried cherries, toasty walnuts, fluffy marshmallows, and toasted coconut bombarded with even more layers, including salty pretzels, savory bacon bits, and a decadent caramel drizzle finished off with a sprinkle of sea salt. The PTA won't know what hit them when you bring these to the next meeting!

- ▼ Cooking spray
- ▼ 1 batch Fudgy AF Brownies (page 36), ¾ cup (138 g) chocolate chips reserved
- ▼ 1 cup (114 g) dried cherries or cranberries
- ▼ 1 cup (105 g) chopped walnuts
- ▼ ½ cup (40 g) unsweetened shredded coconut
- ▼ ½ cup (80 g) Quinoa Bacon Bits (page 14)
- ▼ 1 cup (105 g) vegan mini marshmallows
- ▼ 1 cup (45 g) mini pretzels, broken into smaller pieces
- ▼ ½ cup (125 g) Silky Sunflower Caramel Sauce (page 52), at room temperature
- ▼ 1 teaspoon Maldon or coarse sea salt, for sprinkling

Preheat the oven to 350°F (175°C, or gas mark 4). Line a 9 x 13-inch (23 x 23-cm) baking pan with parchment paper and lightly coat with cooking spray.

Mix ¾ cup of the chocolate chips into the brownie batter; reserve the remaining ¾ cup and set aside. Press the brownie batter into the prepared baking pan and smooth the top out with a spatula until it is flat.

Bake the brownie batter for 25 minutes, remove from oven, and top with the remaining chocolate chips, cherries, and walnuts. Bake for an additional 10 minutes. Remove from the oven and add the shredded coconut, Quinoa Bacon Bits, and marshmallows. Bake for 10 more minutes until the marshmallows begin to puff and brown slightly. Remove from the oven. Top with the pretzels and let cool completely (see Tip).

Once cool, drizzle the brownies with the Silky Sunflower Caramel Sauce and sprinkle sea salt over the top. Place in the freezer for 15 to 30 minutes until the caramel is set.

Cut into 12 squares and serve cold or at room temperature—either way is delicious! Warning: This bar is rich, so don't hesitate to cut each one in half!

Yield: 12 bars

Tip

I'm so impatient when it comes to cooling cakes, brownies, and cookies. Speed up the process by putting the hot pan in an ice bath. Find a pan that's larger than the brownie pan and fill it with ice. Then set the brownie pan on top of the ice. You can add some ice water if there is more room in the bottom pan—just be mindful not to get water on your brownies! You'll have cooled brownies in about 30 minutes. Don't have a pan bigger than the brownie pan? No prob! Fill your kitchen sink with ice and it will work just as well.

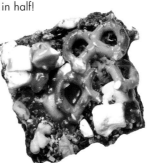

ACKNOWLEDGMENTS

Writing a book is a large task: You start with an idea and hope that people will understand your vision and take it to the next level and then, ultimately, to you the reader. I feel very fortunate to have been paired with a team that did just that at Fair Winds Press/The Quarto Group.

Amanda Waddell and Marissa Giambrone: Thank you for creating such a solid foundation as we hit the ground running and for being open to all of my crazy ideas!

Jennifer Kushnier: I could not have asked for a better partner to tear through the first draft of the manuscript. You challenged me and went for gold—and I loved every second of it.

Meredith Quinn: Thank you for taking us through the finish line with patience and grace.

Chloe Coscarelli: You continue to inspire and amaze me with every endeavor. Thank you for being such a strong mentor, supporter, and dear friend.

My literary agent and publicist, Stacey Glick and Penny Guyon: You see the big picture, and for that I am eternally grateful.

This book would be nothing without the incredible recipe testers who slaved for weeks on end and put up with my insane questioning about every single detail. **Patty Herflicker, Beth Reed, Carla Slajchert, Christine Loeffler, Alison Neumann, Marisa Ford, Rebecca Hess, and Chelsie Davis:** THANK YOU.

LJ Steinig: You once again brought calm to my storm when I needed it most. Thank you.

Elena Beresneva, Joanna Russell, J. Elaine Marcos, and Jonathan Burke: Thank you for lending your beautiful faces, time, and talent to the photos for this book!

Taryn Clayton, Amber Orlino, and Trish Brancale: You came into my life and instantly made it better. Thank you.

Karen Kilgariff and Georgia Hardstark: One might think it strange to thank podcast hosts I've never met in the acknowledgments of my book. But any murderino reading this knows it's not and can identify with my absolute gratitude to both of you (and Steven and ALL the animals) for being with me from start to finish of this book, as *My Favorite Murder* was the soundtrack in the test kitchen. Stay sexy and don't make fun of veganism….and maybe give it a try. Thank you for all you do.

Luciana Pampalone: From the moment I met you, I knew we would have a good time getting these photos done and I wasn't wrong! I feel so blessed to have spent some time with you on this project. Thank you for making me feel and look great in front of the camera!

Ashley Madden: There is no one else I wanted to touch the food photos for this book. I'm thrilled for the world to see your amazing work in this book and with @riseshinecook as it keeps unfolding. Thank you for making the food look epic AF and sacrificing so much to bring it all to life. I'm so lucky to have such a loyal, talented, and dedicated friend.

Sunshine, Tyler, and Dad: Thank you for your support across the miles. I love you all so much.

Mom: Thanks not only for the home-cooked meals that filled the air with such delicious aromas when I was a kid, but also for letting me explore my own taste and creativity. It allowed me to construct the craziness that this book is. I'm grateful for your continual love and support.

Muzzy: You can't read this, but having you by my side in the kitchen is one of my biggest joys. Thank you.

Mr. Rossetti: What can I say? Grateful doesn't describe the way I feel about the unconditional love and support you give to me and express toward my endeavors. You challenge me in ways that make me better, happier, and stronger both in my creative endeavors and in life. I'm so grateful—every single day. Without you, this book wouldn't exist. It's that simple. Thank you, I love you.

A special thank you to anyone who ever watched one episode of *The Vegan Roadie*, clicked "like" on a post on Vegan Roadie social media outlets, took one of my cooking classes, showed up to one of my events and said hello, or bought a copy of *The Simply Vegan Cookbook*. I couldn't have delivered this book without you and your continued support, and I'm forever appreciative for your encouragement as each new project comes along.

Now, get in the kitchen and don't be afraid to play with your food! Keep on cooking, ya'll, and remember: It's nice to be nice!

Dustin

INDEX

ABOUT THE AUTHOR

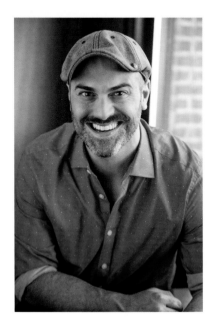

Dustin Harder is the host and creator of the original vegan travel culinary series *The Vegan Roadie.* When not traveling, he works as a personal chef, recipe developer, and culinary instructor in New York City. A graduate of the Natural Gourmet Institute, Dustin has been featured in such publications as *Eating Well, VegNews, Vegan Lifestyle Magazine,* and *Paste Magazine. Epic Vegan* is the follow-up to Dustin's first book, *The Simply Vegan Cookbook.*

www.veganroadie.com

Facebook, Instagram & Twitter:
@TheVeganRoadie